Enriching Arts Education through Aesthetics

Enriching Arts Education through Aesthetics examines the use of aesthetic theory as the foundation to design and implement arts activities suitable for integration in school curricula in preschool and primary school education. This book suggests teaching practices based on the connection between aesthetics and arts education and shows that this kind of integration promotes enriched learning experiences.

The book explores how the core ideas of four main aesthetic approaches – the representationalist, the expressionist, the formalist, and the postmodernist – translate into respective ways of designing and implementing experiential aesthetics-based activities. Containing relevant examples of interventions used in classes, it analyzes the ways in which the combination of different aesthetic approaches can support varied, multifaceted, multimodal and balanced teaching situations in school.

This innovative book will appeal to academics, researchers, professionals and students in the fields of arts education, early childhood and primary education and curriculum studies.

Marina Sotiropoulou-Zormpala is Professor in Arts Education at the University of Crete, Greece.

Alexandra Mouriki is Associate Professor of Aesthetics and Aesthetic Education at the University of Patras, Greece.

Enriching Arts Education through Aesthetics

Experiential Arts Integration
Activities for Pre-School
and Early Primary Education

**Marina Sotiropoulou-Zormpala
and Alexandra Mouriki**

LONDON AND NEW YORK

First published 2020
by Routledge
2 Park Square, Milton Park, Abingdon, Oxon, OX14 4RN

and by Routledge
52 Vanderbilt Avenue, New York, NY 10017

Routledge is an imprint of the Taylor & Francis Group, an informa business

First issued in paperback 2021

British Library Cataloguing-in-Publication Data
A catalogue record for this book is available from the British Library

Library of Congress Cataloging-in-Publication Data
A catalog record for this book has been requested

ISBN: 978-0-367-17932-8 (hbk)
ISBN: 978-1-03-209070-2 (pbk)
ISBN: 978-0-429-05851-6 (ebk)

Typeset in Times New Roman
by Apex CoVantage, LLC

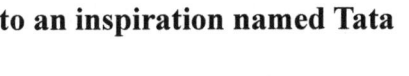

to an inspiration named Tata

Contents

Figures and tables

Flowcharts

Concept map

Tables

1 Introduction

Over the last few decades scholars have come increasingly to consider that the arts must have a central part in curricula. A decisive factor in this has been the fact that the arts have been shown to be adaptable to different and complex educational situations, which frequently constitute the environment in today's schools (Copple & Bredeckamp, 2009; Dailey & Hauschild-Mork, 2017; Parsons, 2004). In particular, and of specific pedagogical interest, is investigating the educational contribution of "arts integration", that is, creating "relationships between learning in the arts and learning in the other skills and subjects of the curriculum" (Deasy, 2003, p. 3).

It has become clear that integrating the arts supports not only the teaching of the arts but also the teaching of other academic disciplines (Burnaford, Brown, Doherty, & McLaughlin, 2007; Deasy, 2002; Goldberg, 2012; Hardiman, Rinne, & Yarmolinskaya, 2014; Robinson, 2011; Scripp, Burnaford, Vazquez, Paradis, & Sienkiewicz, 2013). Examination of numerous instances of arts integration has shown that they can be successful and function pedagogically as transformative zones (Bresler, 2002; Eisner, 2002; Russell & Zembylas, 2007; Upitis, 2011), in which children can explore, discover, interpret, cooperate and exchange ideas during the teaching of every subject.

However, the design and ways of implementing arts integration activities are issues that concern recent research and are of theoretical and methodological interest. More specifically, although there are studies that show a need for arts integration in education to have a theoretical underpinning, they do not point to a structured framework (Booyeun, 2004; Cornett, 2011; Efland, 2002; Eisner, 2002; Gandini, Hill, Cadwell, & Schwall, 2005; Hetland, Winner, Veenema, & Sheridan, 2013; Snyder, 2001; Winner, Goldstein, & Vincent-Lancrin, 2013). Furthermore, these studies do not seem to have examined aesthetics as a basis to design arts integration activities. Yet another issue is the fact that even the studies that have proposals for concrete didactic approaches

(Argyriadi & Sotiropoulou-Zormpala, 2017; Bastos & Zimmerman, 2015; Denac, 2014; Fleming, Bresler, & O'Toole, 2015; Krug & Cohen-Evron, 2000; LaJevic, 2013; Sousa & Pilecki, 2013) do not have a common orientation. For example, using the arts in aid of students' academic improvement is an issue that has divided the research community (Bresler, 2002; Deasy, 2002; Mouriki-Zervou, 2011; Smith, 1995; Winner, 2003; Winner & Cooper, 2000; Winner & Hetland, 2000). Given these issues, both those responsible for the policy of arts education and those who implement arts integration in classrooms feel baffled (Attwood, 2015; Gormley & McDermott, 2016).

From our point of view, coming from the disciplines of aesthetics and arts education, what has concerned us – and this is a concern we share with educators, researchers and theoretical scholars of arts education – is that the integration of the arts in school curricula is being attacked by two sides. At times, the implementers of arts education – frequently individuals who are not specialized in the arts – deal with the aesthetic act as a concept with a loose definition and use activities whose aesthetic nature is dubious. At other times, educators simply do not engage in aesthetic acts because they are intimidated by the arts and believe themselves to be incapable of dealing with them. In this book, we aim to provide a theoretical framework educators seem to need in the first case, and on this basis, we suggest concrete, practical approaches that could encourage educators in the second category to act.

This work contains a specific teaching design for arts integration in kindergarten and primary school. Initially, we examine the theoretical underpinnings of arts integration on key ideas and aspects of different aesthetic theories and approaches. Then we endeavor to organize a structured practice consisting of types of arts activities that correspond to the aesthetic views presented. Finally, the book sheds light on the possible benefits that can be derived when *experiential aesthetics-based arts integration*, as the proposed practice is called, is implemented in school classrooms.

The issue that oriented and guided this study is that arts education could constitute a practical (evidence-based) where aesthetics can be applied to education and where the scope and significance of the "aesthetic teaching" of any subject can be established (Granger, 2006; Macintyre-Latta, 2004; Pike, 2004; Sotiropoulou-Zormpala, 2012b, 2016). This book is based on two assumptions. The first is that every subject taught in school can be dealt with by the children as an aesthetic stimulus. In other words, during the teaching of a subject, children can participate in arts activities that encourage them to explore the aesthetic qualities of the subject and discover its aestheticity. The aesthetic teaching of a subject arises in this way and its content is based on a second assumption: criteria can emerge for the aesthetic teaching of school subjects based on the different approaches to aesthetic theory. The approaches of aesthetic theory can offer different yet corresponding ways of treating the aesthetic stimuli that constitute or emerge from, or more generally are related to, the subjects taught in school. These considerations guide the following study of aesthetic theory as the necessary theoretical underpinning to design and implement arts integration. We examine how each aesthetic approach can be utilized as a base to design respective teaching situations. Moreover, we explore the possibility of a combinatory use of activities based on different aesthetic approaches to create the contents of aesthetic teaching for every subject taught.

We would also like to make clear that in this book, the term *art* shall refer to the processes of all artistic modes of expression: musical/audio, kinetic, theatrical, visual arts, literature, etc., as well as to the arts as a whole. Moreover, the reader should broadly interpret the term, as it frequently refers to activities undertaken by children from 3–12 years old. With this in mind, *art* (and/or *artistic activity*) shall refer to children's engagement with the structural elements of the various arts such as with tone, intensity, timbre and sound in music; movement in bodily expression and dance; colors, shapes, forms, textures and size for the visual arts; facial expressions, roles, mimesis and theatrical objects for drama; and symbolic language in poetry and literature. Based on this, the "arts activities" proposed as suitable for children in kindergarten and primary school are designed to be opportunities for them to use artistic materials and to master "proto-aesthetic" skills.

Following the introduction is a presentation of the theoretical background, in which the core ideas of four main aesthetic approaches (the representationalist, the expressionist/cognitivist, the formalist and the postmodernist/contextualist) are outlined and discussed in connection to arts education theories. It is also critically considered up to which point these approaches can serve the purposes of meaningful and well-documented arts integration practices that appear to be connected to each of them. A section follows analyzing the ways in which the main elements of each approach translate into respective ways of designing arts activities suitable to be integrated in teaching, and indeed in the aesthetic teaching of any subject in preschool and early primary school education. Design models of activities usable with young children are described, and in particular activities which aim to have children participate in learning not only verbally but also bodily, and call upon children not only to respond to aesthetic stimuli, but also to create and/or perform artworks. The next chapter examines the position that respective arts activities can have in primary education. There is then a description and analysis of interventions that took place in kindergarten and first and third grade classes. The purpose of the interventions, the sample of pupils, the manner of collecting data, and the criteria on which the data were analyzed are described, as are the results of the interventions. Finally, the findings are discussed and the educational perspectives are presented in the form of conclusions.

2 Theoretical framework

Until recently aesthetics has been considered rather independent of arts integration in school curricula, and attempts to shed light on why and how to integrate it have been more theoretical than practical (Smith, 2004). University departments of education frequently offer classes on aesthetic theory. However, in these classes future educators are not taught to correlate aesthetic theory with the implementation of arts education activities (Sotiropoulou-Zormpala, Trouli, & Linardakis, 2015; Tarr, 2001). Both generalist teachers – who are overwhelmingly the main instructors in arts education, particularly in primary education (Eurydice, 2009) – and specialized arts teachers do not seem to understand that aesthetic approaches and theories of art, such as representation theory, expression theory, cognitivism, formalism, modernism and postmodernism, are related to the way they deal with arts engagement in the classroom. Despite the fact that "consciously or not, teachers use aesthetic concepts to center curricula in art" (Anderson & McRorie, 1997, p. 6), their use of these concepts is not founded on a firm belief in the necessity to base educational activity on aesthetics. In other words, they do not seek guidelines to design their teaching in aesthetic theory or philosophical theories on art.

This means that although arts education is influenced to a greater or lesser extent by various aesthetic theories (Smith, 1970; Smith & Simpson, 1991; Eisner, 1992a; Parsons & Blocker, 1993; Hutchens & Suggs, 1997; Moore, 1998; Smith, 2004), this influence does not appear focused or systematic. Although the relationship between aesthetics and art education seems to energize current discussion in both the fields of philosophical aesthetics and art education theory (Attwood, 2015; Hagaman, 1990; Mouriki, 2003; Barrett, 2017; White, 2009; Constantino & White, 2010), the research and education community's understanding of this relationship remains either implicit or not overtly addressed (Brown, 2006; Freedman, 2003; Hobbs, 1997) and would benefit from further elaboration. It thus seems necessary to explore how the relationship between aesthetic theory and implementing arts education can become more systematic, and how various aspects of aesthetic theory can be utilized effectively in designing and implementing arts integration at a high level (Sotiropoulou-Zormpala & Mouriki-Zervou, 2018).

This chapter is not an overview of key aesthetic notions or definitions of art from ancient times to the present. Nor is it a survey of aesthetics and/or philosophies of art either – something which is very well done by philosophers and theoreticians of art (e.g. Barrett, 2017; Beardsley, 1981; Carroll, 1999, 2001; Jimenez, 1997; White, 2009). We talk about aesthetics in its broad sense, as that branch of philosophy which critically deals with the arts, but also with natural and cultural phenomena and objects. From this perspective, aesthetics, just like the philosophy of art, examines, studies and formulates theories on art and the concepts connected to it (such as representation, expression, form) and investigates the nature of aesthetic experience that the receiver undergoes in encounters with art, nature and culture (indicatively: Barrett, 2017; Carroll, 1999; White, 2009). In what follows, we adopt the term "aesthetics" and the modifier "aesthetic" because they allow us to refer to works of art, objects and activities, as well as to the manner in which these things are employed and comprehended by children/students.

This chapter is an attempt to single out four main aesthetic approaches (the representationalist, the expressionist/cognitivist, the formalist and the contextualist/postmodernist), and to present the core ideas of each approach and how they are connected to arts education theories (Anderson & McRorie, 1997; Barrett, 2017; Constantino & White, 2010; Fleming, 2012; Sandell, 2009).

We examine the theoretical premises of these approaches, their origin, their different versions and the nuances in their meaning, as well as their contemporary reception and influence. Our purpose is to critically consider up to which point these approaches can serve the objectives of a meaningful and well-documented arts integration process. In this regard, we also refer to the literature about contemporary issues concerning the meaning and usefulness of aesthetics and theories of art, and about the impact of these issues on arts education. Finally, we discuss the ways these aesthetic approaches affect educational practices that appear to be connected to each of them.

2.1 Representationalism

Representationalism is a general term referring to art as representation, as the relationship of an artwork to reality. Some theorists prefer the term realism, considering that the copy theory of art, imitation and mimetic theory, representation theory and representationalism are just different names for the theory of realism (for example Barrett, 2017). Given that a representation is not necessarily realistic, we prefer to use the term representationalism as more general and neutral.

The model of representation in art has a long tradition, which dates back to the appearance of western art up to the present. As an aesthetic theory of art, it seems clear and simple. For approximately two millennia, art has been associated with the idea that it refers to some reality, something outside itself – its subject – which art imitates or represents using its own means. Simply put, even if there is no unified theory of art as representation, what is conveyed in its various versions is the idea of a connection between art and that which it represents. However, from a philosophical point of view, this relationship between art and reality seems to be enigmatic (Fleming, 2012; Mouriki, 2003).

The meaning of representation cannot be looked at in a simplistic way (Fleming, 2012, p. 24) and in order to understand its breadth, one must associate it with imitation or mimesis (as the term has come down from ancient Greece and is defined by Plato and Aristotle) with copying, illusion, realism and representationalism. Beginning with Plato (1974) and the mimetic theory of art, the first and most persistent way of viewing representation associates it with mimesis. From this perspective, a work of art is a copy reminiscent of the original because of its resemblance to it. As has been demonstrated, however, this view cannot be generally applicable. To begin with, it cannot be applied to at least one form of art, music (except perhaps in instances of descriptive or program music). It cannot always be applied to depictive forms of visual art either. Usually to accept that a painting represents something means that we accept a relationship between two existing things, of which one is a faithful depiction of the other. There are instances in which this cannot be: depictions for example of the abduction of Europa, an event that never took place. Despite the fact that in these instances something (whether real or imaginary) is being depicted, one cannot talk about an accurate depiction, about mimesis, or copying, as the supposed original – of which these depictions would be copies – does not exist. Furthermore, what is depicted cannot be identified with its depiction. For example, in religious painting, there are many depictions of the Holy Spirit as a dove. However, what is depicted on a painted surface (dove) refers to something (Holy Spirit) with which it cannot be identified. Even in instances of depicting existing/real persons or things, representations cannot be considered to constitute a copy, the mimetic reproduction in terms of all their aspects or dimensions to such a degree so as to create an illusion that one is dealing with the thing or person itself (Goodman, 1976; Gombrich, 2000).

For these reasons, imitation as the standard way to conceive the relation between art and reality has been challenged. It has succumbed to a more general theory of representation, which would accept as works of art all those works which could be related to something they stand for, whether they look like it, or are realistic, or not (Carroll, 1999; Charlton, 2016; Fleming, 2012; Reid, 1969). In any case, as various conventionalist theories maintain, works that are recognized as realistic are not representations with a consistent or "natural" relation to their object. Their relationship is mutable, depending on visual habits or on customary (in a particular period) systems of representation or on the quantity or relevance of information recorded in them (Abell, 2006; Kulvicki, 2006; Lopes, 1996; Newall, 2011). In this approach, art representations, rather than rendering views or parts of the world and reality more or less faithfully, are bent more towards reorganizing and/or constructing (on a symbolic level) reality (Goodman, 1978), cultivating understanding and ways of seeing the world (Kieran, 2005).

Neo-representational theory – a term proposed by Peter Kivy (1997) and Noël Carroll (1999) – moves along similar lines: in order for something to be considered a work of art, it must be about something, it must have a subject about which it makes a comment. Even if it does not look like what it depicts and/or does not represent something in the conventional sense of the word, a work of art necessarily possesses the property of *aboutness* – it has semantic content and calls upon the viewer to interpret it in order to comprehend it (Danto, 1981).

The theory of art as mimesis or representation corresponds to the learning theory, which has been called mimetic behaviorism: "Art is imitation, while learning is by imitation" (Efland, 1990a, p. 14). Precisely because of this quality, at least in its traditional version, this approach puts students' expressiveness on the margins, and treats them as "imperfect adults", incapable of creative thinking and acting (Blocker, 1979; Richardson, 1992), who must be filled with prepared and controlled information (Tarr, 2001).

Teaching practices based on mimetic behaviorism have been characterized as "didactic art" or "predetermined art" – due to the predetermined nature of the outcomes (Barnes, 1987; Herberholz & Hanson, 1995). The method used in these practices is teacher-centered and the corresponding lessons highly structured. Teachers offer students models to copy in a learning environment that they control (Spidell-Rusher, McGrevin, & Lambiotte, 1992); they determine what the subject is and how it will be taught, aiming at the acquisition and improvement of specific skills (Efland, 1990a); they prepare, guide, control and assess the process and students' performance based on standardized patterns and prepared outlines (Barnes, 1987; Bresler, 1992; Herberholz & Hanson, 1995; Spidell-Rusher et al., 1992).

Although this theory and relevant teaching practices have weathered a plethora of critiques due to their supposedly creation-restricting character and the fact that they undermine children's self-confidence (Barnes, 1987), mimetic behaviorism remains a significant tendency in arts education and its contribution must not be ignored. Its usefulness has been noted by Eisner and other scholars who have written on the significance of using forms of representation (Eisner, 1992b; Martin & Schwartz, 2014). Representing, as Eisner aptly remarks (1992b), makes it possible to stabilize thoughts and feelings, to reflect on what has been represented, to invent or discover ideas and images that were not necessarily present at the beginning of the representational activity.

Other scholars have also noted that the meaning of "mimesis" can have a much richer content and significance than we tend to recognize today (Cannatella, 2008; Fleming, 2012; Rollins, 2001), since it may have a cognitive as well as aesthetic value (Barrett, 2017). As early as the 4th century BCE, Aristotle had already acknowledged that besides aesthetic pleasure, mimetic art had great learning and cognitive value: "people enjoy looking at images, because through contemplating them it comes about that they understand and infer what each element means" (Aristotle, 1995, IV, 1448b 4,5). In other words, representationalism is the aesthetic approach that focuses on recognizing and comprehending the subject of a work of art and interpreting its content (Cannatella, 2008). This is one of the approaches we adopt in this work, the one that will lead to designing representationalism-based arts activities in a later chapter.

2.2   Expressionism/cognitivism

Representationalist approaches examine art more from the perspective of the object/artwork and consider that it reflects states of the external world. As an answer to this view, expressionist theories, which historically succeeded the representationalist (although they did not replace them completely, as seen previously) turned toward the individual who creates and/or perceives the art work as a reflection of his/her inner states (Barrett, 2017; Eaton, 1988; Fleming, 2012; Hospers, 1969).

According to the expression theory of art (which dates back to the 19th century and the romantic movement), what is being expressed through works of art is mainly emotional experiences, that is, the unique feelings of an individual (the artist) who communicates them through a particular medium to other individuals (the recipients of the artwork). Tolstoy's (1897/1964) definition of art at the turn of the 19th century, which greatly influenced artists and theorists, is well known: "Art is a human activity consisting in this, that one man consciously by means of certain external signs, hands on to others feelings he has lived through, and that others are infected by these feelings and also experience them" (p. 10). This is a particularly attractive, yet simplistic, version of expressionism. As has been shown, it is not at all necessary that what drives an artist to create a work is a particular emotion – such a statement would be inadequate and would constitute a genetic fallacy (Dickie, 1979; Eaton, 1988; Hospers, 1969). But even if this is the case in some instances, it does not follow that the feelings can be conveyed directly to and be re-experienced by the public to which the artist addresses him/herself, in the same way the artist experienced them (Dickie, 1979; Fleming, 2012).

Furthermore, as prominent philosophers (Collingwood, 1958; Croce, 1902/1994; Langer, 1953) pointed out later on, art does not express only feelings and emotions, but also ideas. As Langer puts it (1953), the value of art lies in its ability to symbolize the life of emotions (in its broadest sense, meaning everything that can be felt, from physical sensation to intellectual tensions) and express its form. Art is thus the "expressive form" or "significant form" that constitutes the objectification of the subjective reality of feelings. It creates perceptible forms that function as symbols whose significance we conceive out of the frame of discursive language. Expression in art can function as the kind of intuitive knowledge about which Croce spoke (1902/1994) and which allows us to make our feelings clear and thus arrive at a kind of self-understanding. This approach to expression theory comes closer to the cognitive theory of art, which holds that art helps provide knowledge (Freeland, 2001).

It is on this basis that Dewey (1934) developed his pedagogical view, according to which art connected with knowledge is considered a form of insightful cognition; it can offer ways of perceiving the world through individual, complete and unified experiences (Booyeun, 2004; Dewey, 1934). In a similar way, Goodman (1976) defended the cognitive function of art, maintaining that works of art, just as scientific theories, construct worlds. Through this construction, they alter our modes of perceiving and interacting with the world around us.

It seems that the core of the most widespread version of the theory of expression is the belief that art has the ability to make manifest subjective, internal, intellectual situations. The corresponding models in arts education are based on Rousseau's *Emile* (1762/1921), where the author maintains that children have their own ways of thinking and expressing themselves that adults should support. More recently, this view has fascinated many philosophers and arts education theorists of the 20th century. Scholars such as Dewey (1966), Read (1956) and Lowenfeld (Lowenfeld & Michael, 1982) claimed that art is a subjective expression and that works of art are products of the externalization of the child's feelings and emotions, as well as of his/her ideas and views. Along these lines, arts education serves the necessity of a spontaneous, unmediated expression of the child's inner self. Indeed, the starting point for all education should be children's inner powers and instincts, and the focus of education should be facilitating the expression of the child according to his own level of thinking, feeling and perceiving.

It is these views that several expression-centered models rested upon: the expressive-psychological model of arts education (Efland, 1990a), the creative self-expression model (Herberholz & Hanson, 1995), the romantic-expressive approach, the child-centered education (Burton, 2000; Dorn, 2000; Henry, 2002; Jeffers, 1999; Rasanen, 1997). The role of the teacher, according to these models, is non intervesionist: he/she observes, acknowledges and responds to the individual needs of every child separately. These expression-centered models have been willingly adopted by arts educators as they seemed to be based on something very simple and self-evident: everyone, even small children, can feel, express and communicate emotions.

Intense criticism followed hard on the wake of this belief. Doubts about the expression-centered model appeared as early as the 1960s, and criticism was launched as to the extreme focus on the individual. The overestimation of the individual's uniqueness and of his/her right to self-expression was considered "a mania of our day and our culture" (Manzella, 1963, p. 22). This critical stance reflected a more general concern with the exclusive use of child-centered methods of education and the emphasis given to the spontaneous, unreflective and undisciplined free expression in arts education (Chapman, 1982; Entwhistle, 1970).

A need thus arose to reorient arts education. There was a shift to "aesthetic cognitivism" (Alperson, 1991), and models were proposed that aimed to advance the cognitive abilities of children. The arts started to be seen "as the fine vehicles of human understanding" (Abbs, 1996, p. 70), cognitive at their core and inherently of value (Davey, 1989). That is how cognitivist models of arts education emerged which, in great part, were grounded in aesthetic theories such as Dewey's and Goodman's, who, as we saw previously, maintain that experiencing art is essentially cognitive. Under the influence of these views, a group of researchers at Harvard – Gardner and Perkins are the most prominent among them – with the cooperation of Goodman himself, wrote a famous report about the "Basic abilities required for understanding and creation in the arts" (Goodman, Perkins, & Gardner, 1972) and set the basic principles to define cognitively oriented plans for arts in education, which aimed to cultivate creative thought and learning.

It thus seems that, approached from the expressionist/cognitivist point of view, art can not only constitute an expression of emotions, but also broaden one's ability to understand. Creative occupation and encounters with the arts connect to one's inner self, lead to activating interpretative processes and transform one's ways of perceiving (Greene, 2001; Mouriki-Zervou, 2011). Consequently, art can also be a valuable source of learning: the way in which children engage with the meanings embodied in artworks (theirs and others') triggers their cognitive powers and enlivens emotions and thinking. Through their engagement with expressionist/cognitivist arts activities, the children learn to transform their feelings (in the broad sense of the term as used by Langer) into meaning. New dimensions are thus opened for a productive and creative educational process. This approach led us to design expressionism/cognitivism-based arts activities; the manner in which this was done is explained in the following chapter.

2.3 Formalism

Early in the 20th century an approach appeared which disassociated art both from the external world (putting distance between itself and representationalism), and the inner world of the subject (as opposed to expressionism). This approach advocated for the non-practical nature of art, and for the purity of form and its universal acceptance. Its philosophical origin dates back to Kant's *Third Critique* (Kant, 1790/2000) and his claim that form constitutes the proper object of the pure judgment of taste as the essential aspect of beauty. The judgment of taste is associated with disinterested pleasure, which one derives from the simple viewing of an aesthetic object when one concentrates on the form of this object, regardless of any personal, moral, cognitive or practical interest.

The Kantian position on the disinterestedness of aesthetic judgments and the claim to their universal validity are the prerequisites to articulate a formalistic aesthetic, which became the dominant aesthetic ideal in modern art. In analyzing the principles upon which judgments as to beauty rested, Kant certainly was not aiming to form a new theory of art. The fact that a new theory based on Kant emerged was, according to Noël Carroll (2001), the result of a rather selective reading of Kantian theory on beauty by Clive Bell (1913/1958). Bell transported the Kantian concepts of form and disinterestedness into a theory of art and thus launched the most widespread version of aestheticism. Aesthetic formalism was connected to the idea of the absolute autonomy of art and its form, which should be totally unconnected to anything coming from life: "no knowledge of its ideas and affairs, no familiarity with its emotions. Art transports us from the world of man's activity to the world of aesthetic exaltation" (Bell, 1913/1958, p. 26).

In brief, what makes art different from anything else in the world is form. Successful, ingenious and original use of elements, materials and principles of composition, lead to the creation of "significant form" (Bell, 1913/1958). If a form is truly significant it needs no further explanation and its aesthetic purpose is fulfilled unimpeded. Form has a universal nature and can elicit the same aesthetic experience in anyone. On this ground, art is for art's sake.

It "transcends the ordinary by making the experiences of both the artist and the viewer of art extraordinary, beyond the commonplace" (Anderson & McRorie, 1997, p. 9). That is, art is intrinsically important, transcendental in its function, and appreciated for its formal purity (Greenberg, 1961, 1982; Fried, 1998). Consequently, the division between "high" art and other forms of art, between works of art and the products of culture, is absolute.

Formalism was inextricably associated with modernism (Barrett, 1997). It was the theoretical response to the modernist and avant-garde movements that dominated in Europe in the early 20th century. Roger Fry (1920), for example, vigorously defended post-impressionism. Later, the Americans Greenberg (1961) and Fried (1998) were advocates of nonfigurative art, to which post-World War II artists had turned. These critics voiced the view that the history of modern art was a gradual evolution from representation to full abstraction, as the inevitable end for all previous forms of art (Greenberg, 1961).

Despite the robust support and broad acceptance formalist theory enjoyed, it did not remain unchallenged. It was criticized as being ahistoric and indifferent to the social repercussions that art forms may have (Freedman, 2003), and it was considered to have failed in its demands for universality. Although it was used as the most suitable to promote and appraise the achievements of modern art, formalist theory did not succeed in its quest to be confirmed as a general theory on the nature and substance of the art of every era. The obstacle it could not overcome is that, as the history of art itself shows, the greatest part of art has to do both with form and with content. The aesthetic properties of an artwork are not purely formal; they are assessed with regard to how the content is rendered and depend on which category one perceives the work as belonging to (Carroll, 1999; Dowling, n.d.; Feldman, 1992; Walton, 1970). Besides, as Danto points out, an artwork is not to be identified as such by its aesthetic qualities. Something more is needed which doesn't have to do simply with its form (Danto, 1981). But neither does contemporary art seem defensible within a formalist aesthetic theory (Freeland, 2001; Hobbs, 1993).

For all that, formalism has not been completely abandoned. Neoformalist theories (Carroll, 1999), as well as theories of a moderate formalism (Zangwill, 2001), have been proposed which secure a place for content and promote the idea that form and content are related to each other in a satisfyingly appropriate manner.

The formalist view influenced arts education to a great degree in the 20th century and led to the creation of a respective educational model. A great influence in this were well-known educators such as Harry Broudy, who considered the core of arts education to be cultivating sensitivity to aesthetic form (1994). In the same spirit, Ralph Smith advocated the fundamental importance of aesthetic experience (1991). It must be noted that, in reality, neither of these two scholars were bound by a narrow formalistic approach to art which would be limited to noting and describing the formal characteristics of works of art. Broudy devotes a large part of his analysis to cultivating imagination and sensibility. Smith analyzes the complex nature of the aesthetic experience, which does not consist only of being able to discern formal characteristics in works of art, but includes other aspects, such as the emotional and cognitive. The most recognized aspect of their theories, however, remains the technique of aesthetic investigation – the "aesthetic scanning" proposed by Broudy (1987) – as more easily approachable and better able to adapt to the widespread view about formalist arts education.

More generally, formalist arts education demands that children/students develop an ability to concentrate on the internal traits of works of art, on the work itself as form, so as to obtain important aesthetic experiences (Anderson & McRorie, 1997; Barrett, 2017; Hobbs, 1993; Efland, 2004a, 2004b; Feldman, 1992; Freedman, 2003; Freedman & Stuhr, 2004; Hurwitz & Day, 2007). Any other way of viewing works of art that examines them from the viewpoint of the content, the intentions of the artist, or the social, political or moral significance is considered to be of secondary importance. This approach was widespread among arts educators.

Over the last decades of the 20th century, though, an intense critique was expressed against what has been considered as the essentialism of the formalist model (its effort, i.e., to understand art through the quest of its essence, which, in this case, is its form). Critique was also voiced about the insistence of formalism on the autonomy of art (the art for art's sake dogma) and the focus on the universal value of art, regardless of the context in which it is produced and experienced. The formalist approach was accused of possibly becoming exceptionally limiting exactly because it cuts art off from life and, as regards education, from children's reality. The problem with formalist curricula, as noted by Freedman (2003), is not their form but their over-reliance on formalism.

In line with a neoformalist approach, and avoiding extremism, interest in form in arts education curricula can be adopted in a less narrow and more moderate way. With such an approach, form is not disassociated from content, while the contribution of investigating aesthetic traits in order to more fully comprehend a work of art is recognized. Value is placed on children acquiring authentic aesthetic experiences that lead them not away from but toward a more substantive contact with life and their world (Efland, 2004b; Gude, 2008, 2013; Sandell, 2009). This is the manner in which we have approached the formalist foundation of arts integration activities (see next chapter).

2.4   Postmodernism/contextualism

If the previous approach was characterized by its formalist orientation and associated with artistic modernism, over the last decades of the 20th century a relativist-postmodernist approach has arisen. This approach is defined not through a particular, distinct trait, but mainly through an intensely critical stance vis-à-vis the essentialism of the formalist theory and a contradistinction to the central assumptions of the modernist paradigm. Postmodernism promoted variety in art, and proclaimed a new form of belief in diversity, otherness and locality as opposed to uniqueness and universality, individual creativity and originality, which constituted the basic motifs and claims of modernism (Butler, 2002; Habermas, 1981; Jameson, 1991; Lyotard, 1984; Shusterman, 2005; Wellmer, 1984; Wolin, 1984; Vattimo, 1992). To the tendency of modernism to identify art with fine or high art, postmodernism responded with an art that mixes with all kinds of aspects of life and culture. For postmodernism, social and political issues, popular forms of expression, fashion, environment and lifestyles became important.

Within this context, art seemed to have lost its autonomy and become incorporated into the broader sphere of culture. The productive example of modernity was replaced by "reproduction" in which the artist is transformed into a bricoleur who collects and arrays fragments of meanings (Pearse, 1992). Artistic creation developed into a strategy of borrowings of forms and images from the past and from other parts of culture. Art was considered to have entered into an age in which everything was feasible and in which it was allowed to follow any possible direction: into an age of postmodern pluralism (Danto, 1992).

The consequences of this development with a postmodern tendency certainly influenced the field of arts education, as well. Postmodernist models of arts education were being formed that attempted to counter both the one-dimensional essentialist formalist approach, as well as the individualism of self-expressionism. As art became more fluid and dispersed into the broader sphere of culture, it became more difficult to determine the goals of artistic engagement in school. Proposals were made in which arts education should be incorporated into the general framework of cultural studies and more specifically, with regard to the visual arts, into the study of images or "visual culture" (see indicatively: Duncum, 2001, 2002a, 2009; Freedman, 2003; Tavin, 2005; Tavin & Hausman, 2004). A convention was thus created in which the most disparate forms of cultural expression could coexist, frequently without the need for any connecting link, and as a result the question arose for some that perhaps we were being led to the end of art in education (Dorn, 2005).

From another point of view postmodernism includes important traits which could be utilized in a positive way in education. As Richard Shusterman phrased it, postmodernism is characterized mainly by "pluralistic openness, . . . contextualism, pragmatic engagement, interdisciplinarity, . . . and concern for the social, political, and economic forces that structure the artworld and aesthetic experience." (Shusterman, 2005, p. 781). Based on postmodernist approaches, arts education can incorporate these elements, broadening its boundaries with new views and fields of interest. The pluralism of ideas, the multimodality of artistic forms, references to the social context and the articulation of new principles (such as appropriation, recontextualization, hybridity) constitute elements that enhance the contents and the practice of arts education (Barrett, 2017; Gude, 2004).

Although there is no consensual theory of postmodern arts education which could function as a model, there is a group of assumptions and hypotheses which can lead to the formulation of goals for arts education. On this basis, the contents of arts education should be reviewed and ways proposed to do arts education differently (Pearse, 1997).

Art is made as a record of the experiences of individuals or groups defined by class, sex, ethnicity etc. and seeks meanings that contribute to the understanding of these experiences. Thus, the artistic process is transformed into a form of social practice which is called "cultural production". In this spirit, those involved in this process – in this case children and students – are considered to be "cultural workers" (jagodinski, 1991). There is thus a need to examine the social, economic and cultural conditions that form this educational process (Jameson, 1991).

This is a reorientation, a shift in focus, from studying and analyzing a work of art and artistic form to examining the context in which the work is produced and received. Through this change of viewpoint, the various movements for individual rights, the environmental movement, feminism, and various cultures which were considered marginal (and of course cultures outside the Western model) have sought and gained recognition, and have acquired power and a voice. The turn toward multiculturalism claims to avoid the dogmatism of the essentialist/formalist views concerning the supremacy of the so-called "aesthetic character" of arts education (Smith, 2002, p. 13). It has contributed to enhancing the field of arts education studies by linking it to all kinds of artifacts and varied cultural practices which through their variety have broadened it and pushed it towards the acceptance of plurality (Anderson, 1997; Efland, 2007).

Postmodern arts education gives prominence to the correlation of art with multiple extra-aesthetic factors. It rejects the emphasis on self-expression in the expressionism-based approaches (Hawkins, 2002) and pays attention to increasing children's awareness of the social and cultural context (Duncum, 2000; Freedman, 2000). This means it emphasizes the contextualist and instrumentalist character of arts education. From this point of view, the models followed by the modernist/formalist approach are criticized because they transform involvement with art into uses of formal and technical qualities. In their place, contextualist models are adopted in which art is valued for its capacity to express something of significance about the human condition, taking into consideration children's daily experiences and future lives (Anderson & McRorie, 1997; Freedman & Stuhr, 2004). The main purpose of these models is to point out the connection of students' involvement in art with their social environment, with the context within which they live, either to examine it (Aguirre, 2004) or to change it (Anderson, Gussak, Hallmark, & Paul, 2010; Duncum, 2001; Freedman, 2000).

Despite the unquestioned educational significance of these contextual models, no one could claim that they in and of themselves correspond to the demand for a comprehensive arts education. Focusing exclusively on the context and the examination of the social environment, they somehow risk leaving out goals that could not be achieved otherwise but through an introduction of children to the world of aesthetic experience.

There have been proposals of combining approaches and models to counter the unilateralism of the culture-oriented models. Such proposals endeavor to offer a more integrated view of arts education with regard to its purpose and the benefits it might provide for students (Anderson & McRorie, 1997; Efland, 2004b; Sandell, 2009). The proposals do not ignore the role of the pluralist, contextualist vision of the postmodern approach, which can connect art and works of art with the context in which they were created. They also incorporate the vision of the aesthetic experience and thus they redefine the purpose of arts education as one of facilitating self-understanding and meaning-making, enabling cognitive achievements as well as cultural transformation and, ultimately, leading to an enhanced quality of life (Anderson, 2003; Anderson & Milbrandt, 2005; Efland, 2004b; Gude, 2008; Sandell, 2009). Below we adopt a teaching practice based on this approach to design postmodernism-based activities.

***

It is clear that the aesthetic foundations and the related models for arts education presented earlier have differing goals and promote different priorities. For this reason, it would be interesting to consider the possibility that, on the one hand, each model could correspond to a different type of arts involvement, and, on the other hand, that combining them systematically could be a basis on which to design comprehensive, multimethod and multifocusing arts education programs. This is what we attempt to do in this study, so that arts education implemented in school acquires a multidimensional, pluralistic nature. Thus, the involvement of children with the arts will help them to adapt to the post-postmodernist or meta-modernist condition of our increasingly complex world (Van den Akker, Gibbons, & Vermeulen, 2017).

3 Designing experiential aesthetics-based arts integration practices

The previous chapter discussed basic concepts and elements of representationalist, expressionist/cognitivist, formalist and postmodernist/contextualist aesthetic approaches. This chapter examines how these concepts can be used educationally, that is how they can be the theoretical foundation of activities suitable for integration in teaching any subject in preschool and the first grades of primary school. This seems possible if one accepts the view that an individual can develop different criteria to respond to aesthetic stimuli corresponding to different approaches of aesthetic theory (Barrett, 2017).

To an extent, the selection of aesthetic approaches was random, as any could function as a basis to design activities in the manner the four selected approaches did. However, there was purpose behind selecting these particular approaches because of the differences among them, so as to design activities with respectively diverse axes of personal engagement and dialectical interaction on the taught subject (Sandell, 2009). From such a basis, it is more likely that activities will arise which, when combined in the teaching of any subject, can cover a broad spectrum of manners of learning, develop multipurpose teaching approaches, lead to multiple focuses of children's interest, and provide varied ways in which children can use art. Next, the general characteristics that correspond to all the activities being designed are examined, regardless of their theoretical foundations. Following this, the discrete characteristics are examined that match the activities based on each aesthetic approach.

3.1 General characteristics

Activities examined as "arts activities" must be designed so that they are opportunities for children to approach the subjects they are taught using one or more of the art fields. More specifically, the children should be given opportunities to produce and/or perform and/or perceive and/or respond to artworks on the subject (Fleming et al., 2015; Gandini et al., 2005; Tarr, 2001; The College Board, 2013). The activities must create conditions in which the arts, integrated into the teaching of a subject, encourage children to engage in multiple semiotic means (Cope & Kalantzis, 2015; Hesterman, 2013; Kress, 2010). In practice, with regard to the art disciplines provided for by most primary curricula internationally (Eurydice, 2009; The National Coalition for Core Art Standards, 2013), the activities can be:

- musical and encourage children to engage in acoustic tones, rhythms, melodies, musical expression, playing musical instruments etc.
- kinetic and encourage children to engage in moving in space, rough or subtle movement, bodily expression, choreography etc.
- visual and encourage children to work with colors, shapes, forms, textures, dimensions, using materials, artistic expression etc.
- theatrical and encourage children to engage in expressions, roles, mimicking, working with theatrical objects, writing skits, dramatization etc.
- literary and expose children to myths, stories, rhymes, expressing themselves through poetic, prose, or symbolic words, or
- a combination of the above.

As "arts integration activities" they must be designed so as to be adaptable in teaching the subjects of the curriculum (Baker, 2013; Bresler, 2007; Burnaford et al., 2007; Catterall, 2002; Chapman, 2015; Cornett, 2011; Goldberg, 2012; Goldsmith, Hetland, Hoyle, & Winner, 2016; Hardiman et al., 2014; LaJevic, 2013; Scripp et al., 2013), and as such they must be:

- able to be implemented in the conditions of a typical school classroom, without requiring particular spaces or equipment
- able to be implemented by the generalist teacher of the class, that is, they must not require specialized artistic skills on the part of the teacher and
- suitable for all children as part of the general compulsory school education, and not only for those who demonstrate particular aesthetic skills.

From another viewpoint, the activities must be designed so as to contain both a discursive and an experiential part. That is, they must provide the participants with the opportunity to alternate and connect the act with thinking about the taught subject (Bruner, 1977; Cazden, 2005; Flewitt, 2013; White, 2009). In other words, the arts integration activities must constitute fertile ground for interaction between body and mind (Cope & Kalantzis, 2015; Elkjaer, 2000). They must ensure that children are activated while they are producing and performing artworks about the taught subject, and thus encourage the experiential nature of the learning process. Also, they must intellectually stimulate the children, encouraging participation in informed discourses in describing interpreting, judging and theorizing (Barrett, 2017) about the artworks they are engaged in. Briefly, on a practical level, the arts integration activities must be designed so as to encourage:

- the experiential, embodied, kinetic, sensory engagement of the children in producing and executing artworks related to what they are being taught, and
- their participation in focus discussions in which the children are given opportunities to make observations, explain the meaning they ascribe to an artwork and present their views as they are formed on the taught subject.

Yet another important factor influencing the design of the experiential arts integration activities is their theoretical foundation which, on the basis of the proposal in this research, comes from aesthetics. Thus, the activities take on a design orientation dependent on the aesthetic theoretical approaches discussed in the previous chapter. Correspondingly, the theoretical orientation of the activities can be:

- representationalism-based
- expressionism/cognitivism-based
- formalism-based and
- postmodernism/contextualism-based

In summarizing their basic, general characteristics according to their design, the activities being investigated can be called "experiential aesthetics-based arts integration activities". Based on the theoretical aesthetic approaches which underlie them, they must have the particular characteristics discussed next.

3.2   Aesthetics-based characteristics

3.2.1   *Representationalism-based arts integration activities*

Representationalism-based activities lead children chiefly to considerations about the taught subject's realism. Based on the representationalist theoretical approach, such activities are structured so that children can imaginatively "recreate true-to-life experiences, events, sounds, and images" (Cannatella, 2008, p. 5). In other words, in such activities children recognize and learn what the represented in a representation really is. The representationalism-based activities could be ones centered on the subject being taught, which is at the same time the subject of the aesthetic stimuli the children are called upon to engage with. These activities function as an "entrypoint" perspective which places students directly in the center of a topic, arousing their interest and securing cognitive commitment for further exploration (Gardner, 2009; Garrett, 2013). The children thus engage in the arts, and develop a "quasi-scientific" approach to the taught subject. In order for this to happen, they produce and/or present artworks and/or respond to works of art while processing the knowledge they have gained on the nature of the subject being taught.

In practice, during representationalism-based activities children are guided to produce, recognize and judge mimetic representations of the taught subject. Furthermore, they come into contact with artworks that represent the subject in a way that they can recognize it. Based on their design, the activities encourage children to process and more specifically to memorize, recall, recognize and to present through the arts information about the taught subject. For example, children are called upon to mimic in different ways (sound, body movement, art, theatre etc.) some aspect of the taught subject with their artworks, to recognize the subject in the artworks of their classmates, to observe and retain representations of the subject in artistic works etc. Furthermore, in the focus group discussion included in the activities it is possible to posit questions on the taught subject and/or a relevant aesthetic stimulus, such as, "What is the subject? Where is it located in space, time, the environment? Which aspects of the taught subject can one see in the artwork? What do the children know about the subject they recognize in the artwork? What do they observe about the subject that they did not previously know? Does it remind them of anything they have seen or experienced? Have they seen other works on the same subject?"

The following flowchart (Flowchart 3.1) attempts to depict the flow followed to design representationalism-based arts integration activities. As can be seen, elements of the representationalist theoretical foundation are used which correspond to pedagogical aims. Following this, educational practices are proposed that are deemed suitable to achieve the aims. Finally, indicative models of representationalism-based arts integration activities are described. In parentheses in the descriptions are some examples of implementations to show that the activities being described can constitute models for countless variations (depending on the subjects into which they will be integrated, as well as their degree of difficulty). There was an effort in the following models to use the variety of the fields of art that are included in most curricula worldwide (Eurydice, 2009; The National Coalition for Core Art Standards, 2013), that is, music, bodily expression, drama, the visual arts, literature and the artistic use of technology.

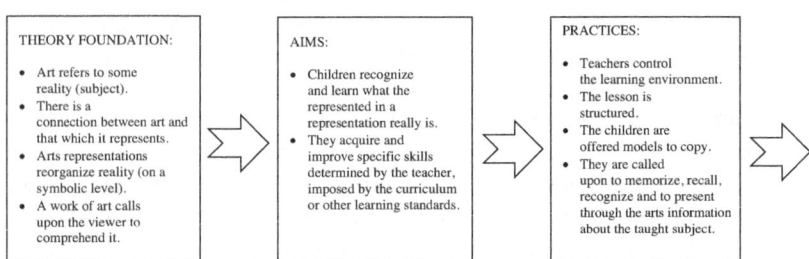

THEORY FOUNDATION:	AIMS:	PRACTICES:
• Art refers to some reality (subject). • There is a connection between art and that which it represents. • Arts representations reorganize reality (on a symbolic level). • A work of art calls upon the viewer to comprehend it.	• Children recognize and learn what the represented in a representation really is. • They acquire and improve specific skills determined by the teacher, imposed by the curriculum or other learning standards.	• Teachers control the learning environment. • The lesson is structured. • The children are offered models to copy. • They are called upon to memorize, recall, recognize and to present through the arts information about the taught subject.

INDICATIVE MODELS:

- Audio environment: Without prior knowledge of what the taught subject is (e.g. means of transport), children listen with closed eyes to a series of sounds of means of transport, either produced by the educator, or recorded (e.g. car, airplane, bus). Based on this stimulus, the children recognize the subject they will be taught and write a text on the knowledge they have on the subject.
- Walking: Rhythmical music plays. The children disperse in the space and walk in step with the rhythm, portraying different attitudes and characters that are named by the educator and are related to the taught subject (e.g. as if they were tired, brave, elderly).
- Choreographies: The children portray words related to the taught subject in movement. Music then plays. The educator calls out one of the words and the children make the corresponding movement in time with the music until the teacher calls out the next word.
- Descriptive movements: The children stand up. The educator reads a taught text, uttering each sentence and including a pause at the end of each one. During the pause, the children adopt a bodily stance and facial expression to portray what they heard. The educator photographs the group. In the end, all of the photos are presented and children retell the text.
- Descriptions: The children and educator stand in a circle and throw an imaginary ball to each other. Every time the ball is thrown, the person who throws the ball calls out a word related to the taught subject (e.g. in a class about Egyptian civilization, the words could be "Pharaoh", "pyramids", "Nile").
- Image making: Children copy the taught text, replacing as many words as they can with drawings. Afterward, they are called upon to read the text of one of their classmates.
- Contrasts: Every child has an A4 piece of paper divided into two. They are called upon to distinguish two opposite elements of the taught subject (e.g. work-vacation, whisper-loud, city-village) and to draw on the two parts of the paper. The drawings are talked about.
- Matching: Visual material is presented (photos and works of the visual arts) related to the taught subject. Following this, a series of recorded sounds which correspond to the works, but are in a different order, are heard. The children are called upon to collaborate to match the images to the sounds. When they finish, the images and sounds are presented concurrently.

Flowchart 3.1 Designing of representationalism-based arts integration activities

Similar flowcharts can be found at the end of the design process of each of experiential aesthetics-based arts integration activities.

3.2.2   *Expressionism/cognitivism-based arts integration activities*

The activities designed based on the expressionist/cognitivist theoretical approach lead children to considerations about the meaning of a taught subject. Such activities contribute to fulfilling an innate human need, that is, artistic engagement being employed as expression (White, 2009). These activities could have to do with ascribing meanings to the taught subject, and be oriented to an emotional and interpretative approach to it (Vygotsky, 2004; Heron, 1992, 2009). Children's participation in activities with such a foundation ensures that engaging artistically is an opportunity for alternative types of understanding and assigning meaning to the taught subject (Dewey, 1934; Efland, 2002; Eisner, 1976, 2002; Goodman, 1976; Greene, 2001; Langer, 1953). The children discover and name what emotions arise in them from the subject they are learning about and develop metaphorical thoughts and perceptions. In this way, they incorporate creative elements into the taught subject and expand their perception of it. In the situation created by expressionism/cognitivism-based activities, children utilize the arts to "see the familiar in an unfamiliar light" (Smith, 1991, p. 144) and to grasp meanings with alternative, non-discursive forms (Langer, 1953). These activities must be structured so that children can display their uniqueness and express themselves better (Lowenfeld & Michael, 1982). Also, the interactions among the children become a valuable process because they include the different types of perception that each child brings into the classroom. Students learn from their peers, each one of which presents different views of the world.

Practically, in such activities children should have opportunities, either by creating or by experiencing artworks, to interpret the taught subject and deal with original and personal meanings that it may bear for them. Indicative models of such activities are when children are called upon to transform the taught subject in various ways (audio, theatrical, bodily movement, color, drawing), composing original individual or group works such as scenes, musical works, choreographies, or visual art. In these activities children should be able to use their imagination, personify, move through time or space and use different kinds of materials to interpret diverse situations. They must be able to create original works without rules from the teacher. Also, during these activities, children must be provided with opportunities to analyze the meanings ascribed to a work of art related to the subject, either by the creator of the work, or the children themselves. In order to make this feasible, the activities must provide opportunity for internal dialogues and/or focus group discussions. The content of these would be analyzing the emotions and meanings expressed by every creator of a work of art that is associated with the taught subject, the experiences of the creator that caused the particular meanings, comparing what meanings were given to the subject by many creators (classmates), the feelings and meanings brought out by the work in those perceiving it, and/or other relevant subjects that arise from the needs of every student and the class as a whole.

The following flowchart (Flowchart 3.2) attempts to present the flow from the theoretical foundation to the creation of indicative models of the expressionism/cognitivism-based arts integration activities.

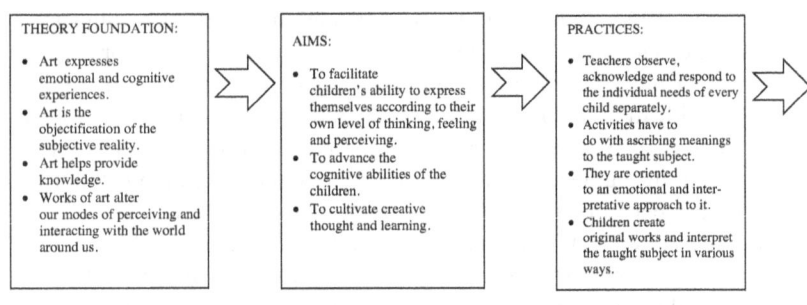

INDICATIVE MODELS:

• Journeys in time: Children create skits about the taught subject, but as if the events take place in a different time in the past or future (e.g. in a class about the *Odyssey*, the children imagine that Odysseus lands on Ithaca today). The skits are performed and commented upon.
• Journeys in space: Same as above, but the skits take place in a location different to the one in the taught subject.
• Transforming objects: Children hold an object related to the taught subject and are called upon to use it in bodily expression as if it were something else (e.g. in a class on writing, they hold a pencil and transform it into a flower, or a flute etc.).
• Role reversal: The children create a skit on the taught subject, reversing the roles of the people involved (e.g. in teaching about the family, the children play the parents). The skit is performed.
• Animating the inanimate: Inanimate elements of the taught subject (e.g. night and day) acquire a voice, personality, manner of moving and behaving, and are included in theatrical scenes which the children make up and perform.
• Chorus: The children choose five key words which in their opinion summarize the significant meanings they themselves have ascribed to the taught subject (e.g. five figures characterizing a taught historical period). They are divided into five groups constituting the "voices" of a "chorus". Each group has one word, and in collaboration with the other groups, decides how they will sing their word (in terms of volume, pitch, intensity etc.). The teacher, in the role of conductor, shows the order in which each word is sung and coordinates the singing. A musical work on the taught subject this thus created.
• Drawing: Each child draws some of the key words of the taught subject. The works are put together with the words and make up an illustration which the particular group ascribes to what they were taught.
• Poetry and music: The children are called upon collectively to compose a rhythmic and rhyming text or poem on the taught subject. They then set it to music and sing it.

Flowchart 3.2 Designing of expressionism/cognitivism-based arts integration activities

3.2.3   Formalism-based arts integration activities

The aesthetic teaching activities that are based on formalist theory lead children to considerations having to do with the aestheticity of the form of the taught subject and its representations.

These activities provide children with opportunities to adopt aesthetic responses and more generally develop an aesthetic attitude toward the subject (Broudy, 1994; Smith, 1991). Based on the formalist view, the activities must encourage children to approach representations of the subject as "significant forms" (Bell, 1913/1958; Langer, 1953) and have relative aesthetic experiences (Barrett, 2017). In the formalism-based activities, children seek the aesthetic elements of the subject and the manner in which these elements are composed into a whole. Originality in children's art-works is praised, as is individuality in the usage of materials and techniques of composing aesthetic works. The children are encouraged to feel freed from the necessity to relate the aesthetic stimuli with reality or with meanings and feelings, or with moral or social values. Participating in these activities, children play games having to do with the form of the subject and the compositional or abstract qualities with which it is imbued. In the spirit of "art for art's sake" these games are not used in a utilitarian way, but rather in an autotelic manner, offering satisfaction because they are experienced as games. More specifically, the activities create situations in which children investigate characteristics such as aesthetic structure, aesthetic qualities, the variety and purity of forms, motifs etc. and articulate a point of view on these. Thus, these activities can be used in teaching artistic notions and art history, in exercising artistic techniques and in initiating one into "aesthetic response" whose "natural progression" is "art criticism" (White, 2009, p. 101). With these activities children can develop their understanding of art and appreciation skills.

In practice, activities designed in accordance with the formalist views could encourage a rather aesthetic approach to the subject taught and relevant artworks. These activities would encourage children to take part in aesthetic exercises related to the external features of the taught subject, construct artworks using various techniques, materials and styles and comment on the manner of construction and the form of the works. Given the age of the children, the discussions included in these activities are not designed to fulfill the cognitive goals of criticism, that is, to be a sophisticated treatment of art, but they may have some basic characteristics of "a good conversation–fresh, personal, incomplete" (Barrett, 2017, p. 14). The discussions are guided by questions such as: "How is the subject formed and presented in the work? What other works present the subject with common features? What comparisons can be made? What are the structural elements of the work/subject? What elements did the creator use (materials, qualities, colors, shapes, sizes, textures, sounds, movements etc.)? What techniques must one know to create such a work? Are there patterns/motifs? Into how many parts can the work be divided, why? What improvements could be made? In what other ways could it have been presented? What types of presentation have been used (description, abstract, realism, distortion, impressionism, surrealism etc.)? To what aesthetic trend does it belong?"

The following flowchart (Flowchart 3.3) presents the flow from the theoretical foundation to the creation of formalism-based arts integration activities.

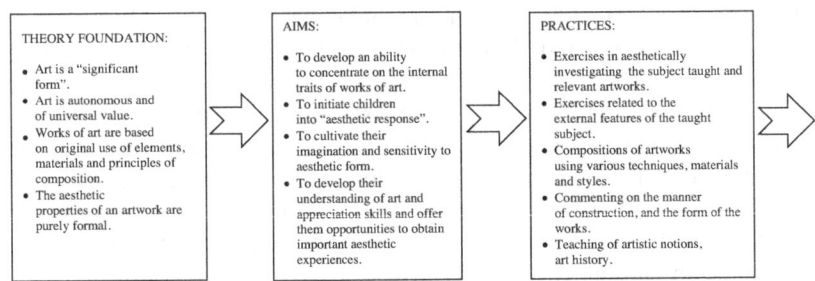

THEORY FOUNDATION:

• Art is a "significant form".
• Art is autonomous and of universal value.
• Works of art are based on original use of elements, materials and principles of composition.
• The aesthetic properties of an artwork are purely formal.

AIMS:

• To develop an ability to concentrate on the internal traits of works of art.
• To initiate children into "aesthetic response".
• To cultivate their imagination and sensitivity to aesthetic form.
• To develop their understanding of art and appreciation skills and offer them opportunities to obtain important aesthetic experiences.

PRACTICES:

• Exercises in aesthetically investigating the subject taught and relevant artworks.
• Exercises related to the external features of the taught subject.
• Compositions of artworks using various techniques, materials and styles.
• Commenting on the manner of construction, and the form of the works.
• Teaching of artistic notions, art history.

INDICATIVE MODELS:

• Works of art: The teacher presents a work of art which she relates to the taught subject (e.g. a painting, a musical work) and gives the children information on the artist, the historical period in which he/she worked, the trend to which the work belongs etc.: the children are called upon to observe in the work the elements they were given information on and to express their critiques and thoughts.
• Types of text: The children are called upon to find and present a text related to the taught subject. The teacher discusses the art of literature with children and teaches them the types of text (poetry, story, narrative, fiction) based on the type of work each child presented.
• Active listening: While listening to a song related to the taught subject, the children are called upon to move to the rhythm when they hear a voice singing and to stand still when only music is playing. The class then discusses the structure of the song.
• Techniques: In a class on a particular subject (e.g. weather phenomena) children try to create an image which requires technical knowledge (e.g. a foggy landscape) on a mural-size piece of paper. During the process, they are taught the necessary techniques, while related works of art are shown.
• Judgment: The children are called upon to express their judgment on the form of art works, either their own or those of artists, that depict the taught subject. The works are classified into groups according to various criteria.
• Fill in: The children paint pictures in which they depict realistically an element of the taught subject. Then, they fill in the painting in such a way so as to make the form of the subject prettier in their opinion (e.g. the grapheme /o/ can be colored in and included in an environment with other /o/ of different sizes, or they can turn it into the sun, or make it into a bicycle wheel, or a face etc.). A discussion is held about the different choices of form.
• Puzzle: The group is divided into smaller teams. The teacher gives each group a piece of a song to sing that is related to the taught subject. A child is assigned to listen to each team's piece and put the teams in order so that the song is heard in the proper order.

Flowchart 3.3 Designing of formalism-based arts integration activities

3.2.4   *Postmodernism/contextualism-based arts integration activities*

Postmodernism/contextualism-based activities are those which, in the aesthetic teaching of a subject, encourage children to concentrate on its contextualist aspects. The activities highlight the social/cultural and more generally contextualist setting of the subject (Butler, 2002; Jameson, 1991; Shusterman, 2005), as well as the plurality of the versions of the subject arising from such a setting. In terms of these considerations "art and aesthetics are too important to be isolated from life" (Barrett, 2017, p. 161). That is, within the context of these activities, children must explore the taught subject and its artistic representations in terms of their social significance, context, history and social conventions (Brouillette, 2010; Duncum,

2000; Elkjaer, 2009; Freedman, 2000; Goldstein, 2008). Using the concept of pluralism (Danto,1992; Shusterman, 2005), these activities protect the diversity among children in a school classroom and allow for the subjectivity each child expresses. Regardless of his/her aesthetic ability, each child deals with a range of modes of expression in order to bring into the classroom elements deriving from his/her own historical and cultural context. At the same time, children are also subject to this type of stimulus from their classmates, which enriches their perceptions of different social versions of the subject in different cultural environments. The plurality of children's experiences finds an outlet in the classroom and their knowledge is enriched and reframed in terms of the sociocultural microcosm contained within each classroom setting. (Gee, 2004; Jewitt, 2009; Gardner, 2009). Expression of diversity, the articulation of the plurality of ideas, observing principles of respect and democracy (Blumenfeld-Jones, 2012) must be encouraged in the communicative environment that develops in postmodernism/contextualism-based arts integration activities. In accordance with the contextualist approach, teaching has to do with the interactions of the taught subject with a network of social factors and encourage a social awareness approach. The artworks analyzed in postmodernism/contextualism-based activities are not divided into pretty or not (as in formalistic activities) but into interesting or not in terms of peoples' lives.

On a practical level the activities are designed so that the taught subjects and the relevant artworks are perceived within the framework in which they function. For this reason, children are called upon to appropriate the representations of the taught subject, manipulate its signs, actively read its messages, combine various cultural elements, reorder the contexts in which the subject is located, and ascertain or revise their views on it (Barrett, 2017, pp. 205–215). In the activities whose theoretical underpinnings are postmodernist, different modes of representation are of particular importance. That is, children are engaged in different fields of art, given that each field corresponds to different facets of the taught subject and arises from activating different sensory systems and intellectual capacities (Kress, 2010; Van Leeuwen, 2015). The value of activities that contain a combination and/or a merging of different fields of art is thus revealed. Indicatively, in activities based on postmodernist foundations, children could be called upon to represent multimodally (scenes, songs, constructions, drawings) situations having to do with the subject in their lives, to create and analyze works related to the existence or nonexistence of the subject, to analyze the role it has played or plays in human lives. The contextualist orientation of an activity could be supported by discussions on the popularity of the subject and its representations, the influence it exerts, and the social aspects of the subject. Indicative questions that could be asked are: "Is the work or its subject popular? Why? What contributed to making it known? How is each student affected by it? How does it affect the rest of the world? Is the world affected on a religious, philosophical, ethical, political or social level? What would happen if it did not exist? Has anyone in the group ever felt a lack of it? Do we do anything about it? Which groups need it most? In what social situations does it appear? What does it mean each time?"

In the following flowchart (Flowchart 3.4) the flow from the theoretical foundation to the creation of indicative models of postmodernism/contextualism-based arts integration activities is presented.

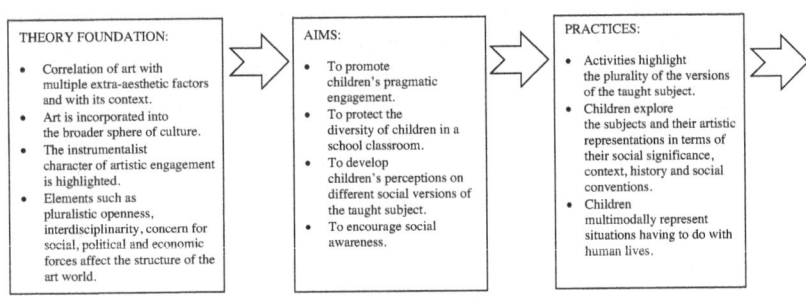

THEORY FOUNDATION:

- Correlation of art with multiple extra-aesthetic factors and with its context.
- Art is incorporated into the broader sphere of culture.
- The instrumentalist character of artistic engagement is highlighted.
- Elements such as pluralistic openness, interdisciplinarity, concern for social, political and economic forces affect the structure of the art world.

AIMS:

- To promote children's pragmatic engagement.
- To protect the diversity of children in a school classroom.
- To develop children's perceptions on different social versions of the taught subject.
- To encourage social awareness.

PRACTICES:

- Activities highlight the plurality of the versions of the taught subject.
- Children explore the subjects and their artistic representations in terms of their social significance, context, history and social conventions.
- Children multimodally represent situations having to do with human lives.

INDICATIVE MODELS:

- Advertisement: The children identify one element of the taught subject which they consider significant for human life (e.g. peace). They are called upon to act like street vendors selling this element and to call out arguments as to why the element is important.
- Detraction: The same can be done with a negative element of the subject (e.g. the war), and the children have to pitch why it must be avoided.
- Plurality of uses: One by one the children hold an object related to the taught subject (e.g. the newspaper) and in pantomime represent different ways it can be used by people (reading, a cone holding fish, light a fire in the fireplace etc.). The remaining children guess the subject of the pantomime.
- Group reflection: The children stand straight and the teacher stands in front of them. A piece of slow music plays and the teacher, slowly in time to the music, acts out different ways in which the taught subject can be used (e.g. in teaching about paper, the movements can be writing, reading a book, wrapping a package etc.). The children mimic the movements. They then comment on the activity.
- Composing versions: The children make a drawing or make a sentence connecting the taught subject to people's lives (e.g. the subject being the sea, the children can draw someone swimming, fishing, gazing at the sea, a boat in a storm etc.). The children's ideas are made into a story.
- Hero: An element of the taught subject (e.g. an element from a language arts text) is chosen by the children to be the hero in a story that they create and which could really happen. The story is performed and this version of the subject is discussed.
- If it happened to us: On first contact with the taught text, the children read until a point and are then called upon to improvise the development of the story as if it happened to them.

Flowchart 3.4 Designing of postmodernism/contextualism-based arts integration activities

4   Implementations

4.1   Why conduct these implementations?

One might wonder about the position that experiential aesthetics-based arts integration activities can have in curricula, that is, about the kinds of teaching situations in which they could have a positive impact. In the following chapters there is an attempt to address this issue. Given that the investigation is still at its early stages, we next explore the possibility that experiential aesthetics-based arts integration activities can contribute to creating the teaching situations for which they have been designed. In other words, we focus on investigating the similarities between the general and specific characteristics that guide the design of these activities (as analyzed in the previous chapter) and the experiences that they expose students to while they are being taught various school subjects.

To begin with, we investigate whether the different approaches to aesthetic theory can be used by students as respectively different ways of aesthetically approaching artworks that they themselves have produced and/or performed and/or perceived and/or responded to. What is being sought is the possibility that the activities being designed based on different aesthetic approaches create a fertile environment for the development of discernable and important pedagogical benefits. If there are indications of this, it would be important to examine the possibility that the benefits flowing from the experiential aesthetics-based arts integration activities based on different theoretical approaches are complementary and encourage an enhanced learning experience.

The study seeks indications of compatibility (or not) between the theoretical bases the different aesthetic approaches offer art education, the pedagogical aims connected to each of them, the practices that are structured to achieve the goals, and the experiences the respective activities create for children in preschool and primary education.

Students' learning experiences are examined when being taught using experiential aesthetic-based arts integration activities, which are designed based on the four examined approaches to aesthetic theory (representationalism, expressionism/cognitivism, formalism and postmodernism/contextualism). In addition, also examined are the possible pedagogical benefits arising from using aesthetic teaching consisting of a combination of activities based on this four-fold theoretical background. For these reasons, some of the indicative models of experiential aesthetics-based activities (presented in the previous chapter as the last stage of the flowcharts) were adapted and integrated into the teaching of various subjects which took place in preschool and primary classrooms. The purpose of these implementations was to show how the students who took part in experiential aesthetics-based activities were affected, depending on which of the four aesthetic approaches was used as a theoretical basis. More specifically, in the implementation of each activity, the following four questions formed the core of the investigation:

- How were the learning conditions involved in the process affected?
- How was the teaching method experienced by the children affected?
- How was the children's focus of interest affected with regard to the taught subject? and
- How was the educational role the children ascribe to the arts affected?

4.2   Who participated?

For the purposes of this study, interventions were carried out with children in kindergarten, and the first and third grades of primary school. In all there were 115 classes, of which 67 were kindergarten classes (938 preschoolers, 499 boys and 439 girls), 29 were first grade classes (696 children, of which 330 were boys and 366 were girls) and 19 were third grade classes (471 children, of which 228 were boys and 243 were girls). The preschoolers were aged from 3.3 to 5.11 years, the first graders were from 6.2 to 6.11 years and the children in the third grade were from 8.3 to 8.11 years.

Convenience sampling was the method used, and the consent of the principal and willingness of teachers were necessary requirements in choosing the classes to be included in the sample. All of the schools follow the current curriculum as provided by the Ministry of Education (Hellenic Pedagogical Institute – Ministry of Education and Religious Affairs, 2003). An effort was made so that the sample included a variety of typical classes. With this in mind, some of the schools were in the urban setting of the capital (Psychiko, Athens), while others were on an island (the broader region of Rethymno, Crete). The sample included pupils in private and public schools. One notable difference between the public and private schools was that the number of bilingual children in the public schools was 16% more. Another was that children in the private schools also took part in non-curriculum classes (sports, introduction to ballet and foreign languages).

4.3 How were the data collected?

The data were collected through participant observation (Emerson, Fretz, & Shaw, 2001). For approximately one week before the intervention the first researcher got to know the children and took part in the daily activities of the classes as the teacher's assistant, so that she was familiar to the children. During the intervention, the researcher used the experiential aesthetics-based activities and the generalist teachers (in a few cases the art teacher) helped as an aide. In cases where the necessary permission for video recording had been given, a spot was chosen for the static video camera in the class. The presence of the video camera was explained in simple language to the children, who quickly seemed to forget it was there. Wherever video recording was not possible, the sessions were audio recorded, provided permission had been given.

In the early stages of the processing, the analyses were exploratory, not based on strict hypotheses and prior theorizing (Collins, Joseph, & Bielaczyc, 2004). Observing repeating patterns in children's behavior helped to determine the specific criteria for the analysis of the data that had to do with the aesthetics-based approach (Sotiropoulou-Zormpala & Mouriki-Zervou, 2018).

On the days the activities were carried out, data of each activity were recorded by the researcher in a specially formulated diary. The researcher wrote a narrative of her general and immediate observations. Corresponding to the research questions, there were four paragraphs for each activity to be filled in. The first paragraph contained observations on the learning conditions in which children were involved. The second contained observations on how children seemed to be experiencing the methods of teaching. The third paragraph contained observations on children's focus on the taught subject and on the emphasis of their engagement. The fourth paragraph included observations on the ways children seemed to be using the arts. A fifth paragraph entitled "Other observations" consisted of comments which had to do with the characteristics of children's experiences in each activity, which were considered important with regard to the purpose of the study, although they were not directly related to the research questions.

When all the activities had been carried out in each classroom, the video and audio recordings were transcribed into text and then subjected to content analysis, after phrases were separated based on content, intonation and the rotation of speakers (Neuendorf, 2002; Rymes, 2016). At this stage there was an opportunity to pinpoint important elements that could not be evaluated in situ due to time constraints. The data collected came from the children's verbal commentary during the experiential part of each activity and the focus group discussion that was inextricably linked to it (Cazden, 2005; Hesterman, 2013; Flewitt, 2013; Michaels, O'Connor, & Resnick, 2008; Morgan, 1988; White, 2009). In the discussions, the researcher and the teachers encouraged the largest number of children possible to speak, asking questions corresponding to the theoretical structure of the activities. Data from the diaries and the transcribed texts were entered on an observational coding grid, which was used as a basis to determine the examined types of behavior.

4.4   How were the data analyzed?

The four questions of this study that make up the purpose of the interventions led to an examination of four respective indicators of children's experience during the teaching process. These indicators constitute the criteria for analyzing the data that arose from the implementations and concern how, in each activity, the children experienced a) the learning conditions involved, b) the teaching methods, c) the focus on the subject and d) the ways of using the arts. Choosing the criteria was guided by the characteristics the activities have, based on their design (see previous chapter). Another guide was children's frequently observed behaviors during pilot implementations that preceded the main intervention. With these criteria as guides, examining the data will shed light on whether the aims for which the activities were designed can be achieved in school practice or not, as, when designing educational practices "saying that 'it is so' does not make it so!" (Allison & Hausman, 1998, p. 124).

The first research question and the respective criterion for analyzing the data demanded an investigation into whether in each experiential aesthetics-based activity the children interacted with "internal and/or external conditions" (Illeris, 2009, pp. 8–10) in relation to the subject being taught. For the former, children's behaviors were sought that were considered to indicate that internal psychological factors, such as their perceptions, emotions and motives were activated to engage in the taught subject (Heron, 1992; Jarvis, 2006). Children's comments considered to be of this type were those which White (2009) calls evocative, expressive, intense, affective; in brief, those which "celebrate the subjective stance" (p. 108). For the latter, types of behavior were examined that showed that children were experiencing processes of interaction between themselves and external-social-environmental conditions, such as the framework within which the subject was being examined, social events, cultural tools and institutions (Brinkema, 2014; Davydov, 1990; Lave, 2009; Wenger, 1998; Ziehe, 2009). White (2009) calls these types of behavior "expository" which "can be very informative" (p. 103) and "they attend to what the students see and feel" (p. 104). These two categories of learning conditions are not mutually exclusive, as a child could, at one stage of an activity, experience internal conditions and at another stage experience external conditions. Thus, the sample was examined twice for each experimental activity, that is, one time for the internal and one time for the external learning conditions.

The second research question corresponds to another data analysis criterion having to do with the teaching methods which, according to the children's experiences, developed in each of the examined experiential aesthetic-based activities. More particularly under examination was whether the children felt they were participating in teacher-centered (Adams & Engelmann, 1996) or learner-centered (McCombs & Whisler, 1997) teaching situations. The children in the sample who were considered to be experiencing a teacher centered-activity were those who were receiving direct instructions from the teacher and were participating in an informational learning environment (Epstein, 2007; Omrod, 2014; Spidell-Rusher et al., 1992). Types of behavior that seemed to indicate this were those that showed children trying to increase their fund of knowledge, to increase their repertoire of skills, to extend already established cognitive structures. Comments classified in this category were those indicating that the educators determined the progress of the activity and that the results of the children's works had to follow the educator's specifications. The children who were considered to be experiencing a learner-centered method were those that seemed to be participating in a humanistic, indirect, self-directed situation (DeCarvalho, 1991; Rimm-Kaufman, La Paro, Downer, & Pianta, 2005; Rogers, 1983; Zevin, 2000). These children seemed to demonstrate that, with the taught subject as a springboard and in the context of a transformative process, they were discovering their interests (Burton, 2000; Dislen, 2013; Efland, 1990a; Goodman et al., 1972; Henry, 2002; Herberholz & Hanson, 1995; Jeffers, 1999; Kegan, 2009; Rasanen, 1997; Upitis, 2011), revising their terms of reference and producing new beliefs and views to better guide their actions (Mello, 2007; Mezirow, 2009). Comments classified in this category showed that the children themselves and their classmates determined the results of the activity; that is, their works did not need to follow the educator's specifications. Furthermore, instances were noted demonstrating that children were taught what they needed and wanted and were self-assessing (Borich, 2007; Burden & Byrd, 2010; Orlich et al., 2007; Wright, 2006). One verification of this process was the diversity of artworks and judgments of the children on the taught subjects. The sample was examined twice for each experimental activity.

The third research question elicited yet another criterion for analyzing the data collected from the implementations of the experiential aesthetics-based activities. Children's comments were sought that indicated their different points of interest in the taught subject. That is, behaviors were sought that showed whether the students focused more: a) on the subject they were being taught (how the subject was defined, what the content was, of what parts did it consist, what its real characteristics were): b) on the emotions and meanings ascribed to the taught subject (by themselves, their classmates and the artist/creators of the artworks): c) on the form of the subject (how the subject and the works of art on the subject are formed and constructed, what techniques were used, what their aesthetic qualities were, what judgments and comparisons arose): d) the real dimensions the subject acquired depending on the context within which it is perceived (how it functions on a social level, what are its different versions, how useful it is, what role it plays in people's lives) (Anderson & Milbrandt, 2005; D'Olimpio & Teachers, 2016; Efland, 2002; Eisner, 1996; Sandell, 2009). These four categories are not mutually exclusive, and thus, in order to collect data on this criterion, the sample was examined four times, once for each kind of focus. First children were counted in terms of their engagement with managing information on the subject (trying to recall, mimic, memorize or recognize the realistic elements of or about the subject, and indeed as these were included in the curriculum); second in terms of their engagement with expressing meanings on it (interpreting the taught subject, ascribing to it personal or collective meanings, and extending it by imbuing it with imaginary elements and/or emotional content); third their engagement was counted as to acquiring aesthetic techniques and aesthetic knowledge of the subject (practicing techniques and revealing knowledge about the structure/construction/form of the subject, making related judgments, using an aesthetic vocabulary); and fourth their engagement in connecting the subject to the social world (social versions of the subject, recognizing its influence among its users and more generally in human life) (Duncum, 2001, 2002b; Efland, 2007; Freedman, 2000; Freedman & Stuhr, 2004; Parsons, 2004).

As to the fourth research question, it was considered important to seek which of the two basic educational roles of the arts, the essentialist role of a taught subject or the contextual role of a teaching medium (Burnaford et al., 2007; Eisner, 1972; Lindström, 2012; Markovic, 2011; Sotiropoulou-Zormpala, 2012b), children used when taking part in experiential aesthetics-based activities. With regard to this, the participants were counted two times. The first time was counted if the children reaped benefits which Eisner calls "arts-based" and are "directly related to the subject matter that an arts education curriculum was designed to teach" (1999, p. 146). Indications of such benefits were considered to be children's engagement with mastering new knowledge of and skills in art, with expressing their aesthetic criteria, fulfilling them artistically, and with comprehending the phenomenon of art (Anderson, 2016; Barnes, 1987; Eisner, 2002; Gelineau, 2012; Griffin et al., 2017; Hetland et al., 2013; Ho, 2016; Narey, 2008; Nathan, 2014). Children were counted a second time when they showed signs of broader "ancillary" benefits (Eisner, 1999), having to do with personal, and academic development through the arts (Deasy, 2002; Goldberg, 2012; Hardiman et al., 2014; Rooney, 2004; Scripp et al., 2013; Hetland & Winner, 2000). This type of benefit was considered to arise when working artistically served goals related to the taught subject, or when children were activated toward these goals, and when the environment of the class was felt to be playful and attractive (Baker, 2013; Bilhartz, Bruhn, & Olson, 2000; Burnaford et al., 2007; Catterall, 2002; Chapman, 2015; Goldsmith et al., 2016; LaJevic, 2013; Lilliedahl, 2018; Luftig, 2000; Rabkin & Redmond, 2004; Robinson, 2011; Webster & Wolfe, 2013).

The analysis criteria of the implementations of the experiential aesthetics-based arts integration activities are presented in the form of a concept map.

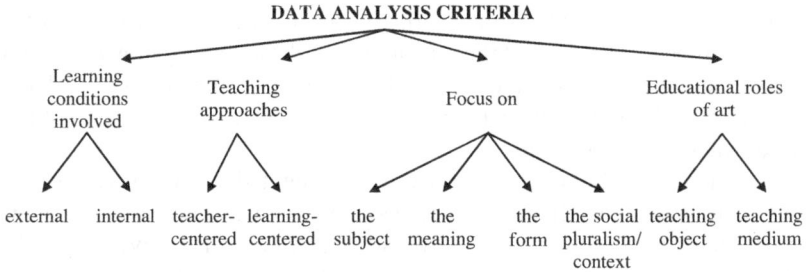

Concept map 4.1 Data analysis criteria

4.5   What was implemented? What were the findings?

The examined experiential aesthetics-based activities were adapted to the teaching schedule of all the classrooms of the sample. That is, the activities were shaped so that they could be integrated in teaching the subject that was being taught in every class of the sample when the intervention took place. Following are descriptions of the interventions which were integrated into six different taught subjects.

More specifically, in the Language Arts syllabus, experiential aesthetics-based activities were integrated into the "parts of speech – adverbs" subject in 19 classes (471 children) of the third grade. In the Mathematics syllabus the activities were used in 67 kindergarten classes and 29 first grade classes (1634 children) and integrated in the teaching of "first single-digit numbers". In the Human Environment Studies syllabus the activities were used with the students of 29 first grade classes (696 children) in teaching about "the human body". In the Natural Environment Studies syllabus activities were used in 67 kindergarten classes (938 children), for the class on "botany-flowers" and another in 67 kindergarten classes (938 children) for "water and the phenomena of the cycle of water". In the Visual Arts syllabus activities were used in 29 first grade classes (696 children) on the meaning and artistic trend of "surrealism". For each subject there were four activities, designed to correspond with the four views of aesthetics discussed previously (the representationalist, the expressionist/cognitivist, the formalist and the postmodernist/contextualist), as being representative of trends that implicitly or explicitly influence aesthetic education curricula.

In the following descriptions, the examined activities are coded with a letter representing which approach they are based on (R for representationalist, E for expressionist/cognitivist, F for formalist and P for postmodernist/contextualist foundation). The number in the code indicates the subject the activity was used for (1 for the "parts of speech – adverbs" class, 2 for the "first numbers" class, 3 for "the human body", 4 for "botany-flowers", 5 for "water and the cycle of water" and 6 for "surrealism"). Each activity has a title that could refer to its general structure, regardless of the class subject into which it was integrated.

The activities for each subject were implemented as a program consisting of four modules. In most cases, each module was implemented in one day. Thus, each entire program spread over four consecutive days. The interventions took place with the collaboration of one researcher and the generalist teacher in each classroom, or in fewer cases, with the art teacher. Each activity was scheduled to last from 20 to 40 minutes, but in practice they were extended by ten minutes at most, only when the children requested it.

The four activities that constitute each one of the six programs are described, followed by the results that arose from the implementations. The presentation takes place in this order: the program of activities used in language arts ("adverbs"), in mathematics ("first numbers"), in human environment studies ("the human body"), in natural environment studies ("botany" and "water – the cycle of water") and in visual arts ("surrealism").

Abiding by the criteria analyzed previously, the results for each activity derived from the members of the sample who were examined separately for every type of behavior considered to be an indicator of the manner in which they were experiencing the teaching. Types of behavior were examined that demonstrated that the children were functioning based on internal or external learning conditions. Also, behaviors were studied that showed children experiencing a direct, teacher-centered or indirect, student-centered teaching method. Behaviors were looked for that showed the focus of interest for the children was on learning the taught subject, or on rendering and expressing meanings on the subject, or the formal and aesthetic dimension of the subject, or connecting the subject to the social world. In addition, signs were sought that children were using the arts either as a taught subject or as a means of teaching.

In the presentation of the results that follows, excerpts either from the transcribed video/audio recordings or the diaries are placed within quotation marks as indicative of each type of experience identified. Each child was counted only once, even if he/she repeatedly demonstrated one of the types of experience being examined. Every type of behavior that was being examined so as to include children in one or another category was judged by its most basic and intense elements. It is worth noting, however, that this process has limitations, because of the fact that every type of behavior is intertwined with others, and its characteristics are never totally clear and discrete. To deal with this to an extent, the work of decodifying and quantifying the data was carried out by the authors and three independent associates.

4.5.1   Aesthetics-based teaching of "parts of speech – adverbs" (Language Arts Syllabus)

a.   Description of aesthetics-based teaching of "adverbs"

In the aesthetics-based teaching of "parts of speech – adverbs" the following activities were used:

R.1. PHYSICALLY EXPRESSING WORDS

The educator writes words related to the lesson on small pieces of paper, e.g. simple adverbs of time (tomorrow, never, later), place (down, here, anywhere), manner (well, together, secretly), quantity (much, little), frequency (never, often) and adverbs of answer or response (in Greek: yes and no), then distributes them randomly to the children who are divided into pairs. Each pair is called upon to use the adverbs on their paper in a sentence and render the meaning through physical expression, without using words. The educator helps each pair separately, discussing the meaning of their adverbs with them. During the children's presentations, the teacher shoots video and/or takes photos. The theoretical foundation of the activity is **representationalist**.

F.1. CRITIQUE

The audio-visual material from the previous exercise is then presented and the children in the class are called upon to name each pair's word (adverb). The children discuss the kinetic ways in which the subject is portrayed. They give ideas on how to improve the manner of expression (movements, facial expressions). The theoretical foundation of the activity is **formalist**.

E.1. CREATING A SKIT

The activity continues and, as a group, the children choose four of the words already used (four adverbs) and are asked to work together to connect them in a brief skit and perform it. A discussion follows on the meaning of the skit. The theoretical foundation of the activity is **expressionist/cognitivist**.

P.1. VISITOR

In the last stage of this program, the children invite the teacher of another classroom in to present the works they created on adverbs. They exhibit the photos, organize the presentation of parts of the video material and present the theatrical events they created in the previous activities. During the presentations, each child explains the work he/she has created and discusses his/her views on the taught subject. Comparisons are made and differences in perceptions are underlined. The theoretical foundation of the activity is **postmodernist/contextualist**.

b.   Results of aesthetics-based teaching of "adverbs"

How the third-graders experienced the teaching process in activities R1 (Physical expression of words), F1 (Criticism), E1 (Creating a skit) and P1 (Visitor) was examined during the implementation of the program.

During the pantomime presentation of the subject in activity R1 (Physical expression of words), it seemed that the children interacted at times with external and at other times with internal conditions of learning. Indicative of their interaction with external conditions, it was frequently observed that some adverbs were portrayed with common bodily motifs. For example, adverbs of time referring to the future were portrayed with children moving forward. An even more characteristic example of external learning was the motion to render the adverbs of response: most children rendered "yes" by lowering their heads, and "no" by raising their heads as is common in Greece (and different to gesturing "yes" and "no" in other European countries). In terms of internal learning conditions, they rendered adverbs in symbolic motions, particularly in cases that had to do with the children's feelings (for example opening hands to mean "I love you very much"). In the same exercise, most children seemed to be experiencing a teacher-centered situation. Indicatively, while preparing for the pantomime, the teacher gave information, clarified and corrected the children on the taught subject, and at times interfered in the pantomime. For their part, the children frequently sought the opinion of the teacher to ensure that they had properly understood an adverb in the scene they were to present. They were more occupied with the literal information contained in the taught words and more rarely with processing them metaphorically. All this shows that during this activity there were signs that children's basic interest was on the taught subject itself. The children also seemed to use art (pantomime) in most cases as a means of teaching this subject. According to a written observation, "the children were occupied mainly with the literal meaning of the adverbs they were working with, and on this basis sought a suitable body pose".

In activity F1 (Criticism), almost all the children in the sample demonstrated that they perceived the subject mainly on the basis of external conditions of learning, seeking to recognize the contents of every pantomime in terms of the forms of the movements ("she's moving her hand as we do to say 'a lot'", "if she did this, I'd have understood it better"). In fewer cases the children decodified the movements based on feelings or more generally on meanings that they themselves ascribed to the events in the pantomime. It seemed the children frequently experienced this to be a teacher-centered approach and were occupied with information on the adverbs ("why did you portray 'once' like that?", "how do you do 'so'?"). There were more than a few instances in which the children seemed to consider they were taking part in a learner-centered approach, mainly when dealing critically with the bodily motion needed to render the taught subject ("his face showed that he's happy and he likes it"). Almost all children in this activity seemed to be occupied mainly with the form (the shapes of the movements) that the taught subject could take. All the children's comments had to do with the perception of movements and facial expressions as modes of communication. During this activity, the role ascribed to art (analyzing the movements) was mostly that of the taught subject as it seemed the children felt they were being taught bodily expression. The children were occupied with the manner of using expressions of the face and body, and several times referred to their conclusions on the motifs they considered suitable or not, and in other cases expressed conclusions of an aesthetic nature ("when we do our eyebrows like this, it means we don't like it.")

In activity E1 (Creating a skit) it seemed the children experienced learning mainly as an internal psychological condition ("Once, in my imagination"). Fewer references could be associated with external factors; this was thought to be because the activity was not done individually, but had small

Table 4.1 Positive indications (>50% of the sample) for the aesthetics-based teaching of "adverbs"

ACTIVITIES	DATA ANALYSIS CRITERIA									
	Learning conditions involved		Teaching approaches		Focus on				Educational roles of art	
	external	internal	teacher-centered	learning-centered	the subject	the meaning	the form	the social pluralism/ context	teaching object	teaching medium
R.1. Physical expression of words	✓	✓	✓		✓					✓
F.1. Criticism	✓		✓	✓			✓		✓	
E.1. Creating a skit		✓		✓		✓			✓	✓
P.1. Visitor	✓	✓	✓	✓				✓	✓	✓

groups cooperating ("let's not put that, because it's not done that way normally"). During this activity, most children seemed to feel free to assign and express meanings and emotions to the taught subject and to decide as to the development of the exercise (three children on combining 'so', 'not at all', and 'never': "Leave me alone. I like it so!", "I never do what grown-ups want", "Because I care not at all what they say", "I laughed with Yiannis-Josef, I liked what he said . . ., I laughed for 15 hours"). From the children's works, it appeared that they processed the subject in an interpretative and transformational way. Their interest seemed to be focused, in fact exclusively, on assigning and expressing meanings in the taught subject. The role of art (creating a skit, organizing and performing a theatrical scene) was considered to be mixed, as the children seemed to be involved in the meaning of the adverbs, experiencing teaching through art, while at the same time they ascribed aestheticity to the adverbs (enhancing them with imagination, dealing with them multimodally, symbolic/interpretative approach), experiencing a situation with the traits of a drama lesson.

In activity P1 (Visitor) it seemed that the children were exposed to the plurality of views that can be associated with the taught subject, to which both internal and external perceptual factors contributed. There were numerous observations of children repeating the information they had been taught, but also quite a few of children interpreting the information ("they frequently repeated parts of their skits in activity E1"). It seems that the teaching approach the children were experiencing was mixed, including elements of teacher- and learner-centered situations. The explanations the children gave to their visitor revealed that their focus was mainly on connecting the subject with their life experience ("daddy does everything slow and mommy quickly. That's why I do this in the performance"). The art (pantomime, skits, dramatization) in this activity seemed to be balanced between the role of medium and of the taught subject, as some children talked about the literal use of adverbs and some about aesthetically approaching them.

Table 4.1 presents a picture of the results of the program incorporated into the language arts class on adverbs. The positive indications ranging from 50% and above of the sample are presented.

4.5.2 *Aesthetics-based teaching of "first numbers" (Mathematics Syllabus)*

a. Description of aesthetics-based teaching of "first numbers"

The following experiential aesthetics-based activities were designed to be suitable to be integrated in teaching "first numbers":

P.2. A WORLD WITHOUT . . .

Children are asked to imagine a world completely lacking the subject being taught (what their life would be like without numbers). They are then called upon to act out (pantomime, dialogues, theatrical improvisation) the situations they would find themselves in. The presentations are then analyzed in terms of the facets of human life that are influenced by the subject (e.g. systems of counting money, space, time, weight etc.). The theoretical foundation of the activity is **postmodernist/contextualist**.

F.2. HUMAN SCULPTURES

In the next step, the children examine the form of the taught subject and are asked to create representations of the subject by posing as sculptures. The teacher writes down a number and the children pose their bodies, an arm or leg, or with one or more classmates, or with the help of an object such as a chair, in such a way as to represent the grapheme. The result is photographed, presented and compared to the written number. The children then write down their own numbers and are instructed to decorate them (using colors or other materials) without changing their shapes. The theoretical foundation of the activity is **formalist**.

R.2. THE TEACHER HAS AMNESIA

At this stage, after a break, the teacher pretends that a magic potion in his/her juice made him/her forget what he/she had taught. The teacher remembers neither the subject, nor what had been said about it. He/she then asks the children to help him/her remember. In turn, the children play the role of teacher and act as if they are teaching, reminding him/her that the subject was numbers, they repeat the numbers they had been taught, and what they knew about each number. Throughout the process, the teacher pretends to be a forgetful student trying to repeat what the children are teaching him/her, but frequently makes mistakes. The children correct him/her. The teacher has many questions and needs many explanations. The theoretical foundation of the activity is **representationalist**.

E.2. CHARACTERS OF THE SUBJECT

Finally, based on what they learned, the children talk about how they imagine the character of each number and they highlight their favorite. In a group discussion including the teacher, they agree on some prevailing ideas about the way each number walks, what it says, how it talks, what it wears. Based on this, the children produce brief verses and they render them rhythmically and theatrically. The theoretical foundation of the activity is **expressionist/ cognitivist.**

b. *Results of aesthetics-based teaching of "first numbers"*

Activities P2 (A world without), F2 (Human sculptures), R2 (The teacher has amnesia) and E2 (Characters of the subject) were used for the aesthetics-based teaching of "first numbers". The results, presented next, on each one of the activities, follow the order listed here.

In activity P2 (A world without . . .) the children seemed to perceive numbers based on external conditions. Indicatively, they referred to institutions and systems related to numbers ("the way their parents are paid their salaries", "measuring time", "the numbers in their addresses", "sizes of clothes", "measuring distances"). In some cases, a lack of numbers activated internal conditions of learning ("sadness that there would be no more birthdays and Christmas"). Both during the organizing of the dramatizations and during their analysis there were opportunities for the educator to teach information. In fewer cases, children approached the subject interpretatively and imbued the lack of numbers with emotion ("you wouldn't be able to count us and you could forget me in school, or not put me on the school bus, and I would cry"). The focus of interest for most children was the multitude of uses numbers have and the crucial role they play in daily life. Art (physical expression, theatrical activity) was used by the children as a teaching medium, as most of their speech had to do with the taught subject rather than the arts processes.

According to the instructions for activity F2 (Human sculptures), the children interacted with external conditions of learning the subject, and more specifically with the form of the numbers' graphemes. However, in some cases it seems that internal criteria were activated and the numbers were seen as significant forms ("number 1, because it's proud, it has that little line at the top: it's its nose that's pointing upward, just like people who are snobs"). The teaching was rather teacher-centered and had an informational orientation. Indicative of this, even in the stage where children were drawing, they frequently asked feedback questions about their works ("if it's right" or "where they had gone wrong"). The implementer supported this process ("if you put this line in, will we be able to see that it's a 7?"). The center of interest for all children seemed to be the form of the subject ("Yannis' legs are stretched, and Mathos should bend more to look more like a 2"). The visual arts seemed to function as a teaching medium, as the children behaved as one would expect in a class teaching the number graphemes through the arts. However, the children were frequently interested in the techniques of posing like a number and decorating the graphemes – in these cases the teaching had the characteristics of teaching visual arts.

In activity R2 (The teacher has amnesia) the children almost exclusively experienced external social learning conditions. Nevertheless, in some fewer cases, as the children were trying to remind the teacher the content of the lesson, they used meanings that they themselves attributed to the numbers in activity E2 ("don't you remember 1 that we said was all alone and it had no friends?"). Most children seemed to experience the teaching approach as teacher-centered. Although they seemed to be self-motivated and self-activated, they were mimicking the exemplar of their teacher, both in terms of the information on the taught subject ("we're talking about numbers", "put them in order", "no, six comes after 5"), and in terms of the role they were playing ("try to concentrate", "you don't remember?", "come on, it's OK, I make mistakes sometimes too"). The activity seemed to function well for learning and repeating the information the children had been taught ("they frequently interacted when some child repeated information that was not correct"). The taught subject was the center of interest for almost all children ("let's see, can you remember how to write 6?", "count with your fingers"). Almost all the children seemed to see the art (playing a role) in this activity as being a teaching medium. In a playful and theatrical way, the children had opportunities to fulfill the goals of their curriculum on the taught subject ("Try again from the beginning: 1, . . .").

In activity E2 (Character of the subject) the majority of the children activated internal conditions of learning, attributing meanings and feelings to the numbers ("1 is the most hurried and fastest number because it drives in Formula 1"). Although the children were helped by the teacher, they seemed to be having a learner-centered experience in which they felt free to transcend the information they had been taught, personify the subject, and identify with it. Most children tended to augment the subject with new knowledge and transform their perceptions of it (e.g. "number 4 is the number of love of a family that has two parents and two children", "it walks softly and sings in a low voice: I am beautiful 4, the elegant 4, waiting for you, outside your front door!", in another group number 6 was strict and banging its legs on the floor it walked and said: "I am 6, the strict 6, and I'll have none of your tricks. Come rain or come shine, as a 6 I'll give you a piece of my mind!". These examples are translated from Greek and do not accurately render the rhythm of speech and the musicality of the children's works). Also, in this activity the children's interest was focused mainly on interpreting and assigning meaning to the subject. In terms of the role attributed to art (creating verses, rhythmic/musical and theatrical rendering of the verses, coordination) it seemed that most children believed they were participating in an art class. The children were chiefly occupied with the aestheticity of the subject and their works. However, at the same time it was observed that the works of many children were influenced by information related to the subject, such as the name of the number, cardinality, grapheme ("three was a lazy clover that snored like this: 'thrrrrrrrr'", "five was a palm that liked to dance"). These statements were considered to demonstrate that art was being used as a teaching medium.

Table 4.2 presents findings showing positive indications ranging from 50% and above of the sample.

4.5.3 Aesthetics-based teaching of "the human body" (Syllabus of Human Environment Studies)

a. Description of the aesthetics-based teaching of "the human body"

The experiential aesthetics-based activities designed to be used in the aesthetic teaching of "the human body" are as follows:

R.3. THE MOVEMENTS OF THE SUBJECT

The educator explains to the children that he/she was going to show them "various ways they can move the parts of their body". Slow music begins to play, and the educator makes slow movements with one part of his/her body. The children stand across from the educator and mirror his/her movements with the greatest precision possible. The educator accompanies the movements with a verbal description of the movements his/her body can make. Then, in turn, a child takes the place of the educator, while the latter calls out which part of the body to move. In the discussion that follows, the children are called upon to repeat the parts of the body that moved, and to comment on the kinds of movement that each part can make. The theoretical foundation of the activity is **representationalist**.

F.3. RECOGNIZING BY TOUCH

The activity continues with a version of blind man's bluff. The educator calls out a body part and a blindfolded child touches a classmate on that part, trying to recognize him/her. The blindfolded child calls out the particular traits of the body part he/she is touching until he/she recognizes his/her classmate. Every so often, the educator changes the body part. Afterwards, a discussion takes place on the factors that contribute to recognition, such

Table 4.2 Positive indications (>50% of the sample) for the aesthetics-based teaching of "first numbers"

ACTIVITIES	DATA ANALYSIS CRITERIA									
	Learning conditions involved		Teaching approaches		Focus on				Educational roles of art	
	external	internal	teacher-centered	learning-centered	the subject	the meaning	the form	the social pluralism/context	teaching object	teaching medium
P2 A world without	✓		✓					✓		✓
...										
F2 Human sculptures	✓	✓	✓				✓		✓	✓
R2 The teacher has amnesia	✓		✓		✓					✓
E2 Character of the subject		✓		✓		✓			✓	✓

as texture, temperature, the dimensions of body parts, and the variety that exists among different people. The theoretical foundation of the activity is **formalist**.

E.3. DIALOGUES

Each child works individually and is instructed to prepare and present a dialogue between two parts of their bodies, e.g. their hands. They then analyze the meanings in their sketch and the group comments. The theoretical foundation of the activity is **expressionist/cognitivist**.

P.3. RESTRICTIONS

In the last part of this program, a discussion begins on the usefulness of parts of the body, the need for coordination, and the difficulties that arise when they are restricted. As part of the discussion, the children are called upon to try some ideas such as having one arm stuck on their body from shoulder to palm, they are asked to play a percussion instrument, or tidy their crayons in a box, or tie their shoelaces. Afterwards, rhythmical, pleasant music plays in the background, and the children move to the rhythm. They are arranged two by two, having a part of their body (e.g. palms), called out by the educator, touching the respective part of a classmate's body. The body parts change throughout the activity (arms, legs, backs, cheeks). The theoretical foundation of the activity is **postmodernist/contextualist**.

b. Results of the aesthetics-based teaching of
   "the human body"

The results of the aesthetics-based teaching of the "human body" came from the activities, in the order they were implemented R3 (The movements of the subject), F3 (Recognizing by touch), E3 (Dialogues) and P3 (Restrictions) in first grade classes.

In activity R3 (The movements of the subject) it was observed that most children learned based on external conditions related to the subject ("they mimicked the movements of the teacher"), while at the same time they were being given verbal explanations ("the palm is connected to the rest of the hand so that it can make circular movements like this"). Observations such as most children "were focused on the movements of the educator", and managed to "mimic them with great precision" show the teacher-centered and informational orientation of the teaching approach ("Am I doing it right, miss?", "Only shake your head", "The implementer of the activity was asked many questions about the names of various parts of the body such as knee, shin, ankle"). It is worth noting that indications of direct teaching were seen, not only in the children's words, but also from the observations of non-verbal behavior (look, body posture, movements). The main focus of the children seemed to be the taught subject ("what's that called? – Wrist", "I can do it like this, and this and this", "Matoula is moving her ears"). Children's comments showed the care they took in repeating the parts of the body and the manner in which they can move ("they referred to details of the movement", "they corrected their classmates"). Fewer children engaged in self-expression or connected the subject to their own experiences ("he held his hands like a bird flying"). It also seemed that the children were mainly occupied in managing the information on the subject, the vocabulary, and the movement ("I thought that the nose was motionless", "I didn't know that my tongue could reach so far"). In this activity it seems that most children experienced teaching parts of the body through art (mimicking of movements).

In activity F3 (Recognizing by touch) children seemed to use mainly external conditions related to the parts of the body ("long hair", "tall", "nice soft skin"). Most children experienced the lesson as teacher-centered and informational during which "they were called upon to find a correct answer as to the classmate they'd recognized" and "the class teacher praised correct and fast recognition". Some of the class teachers commented on the "precise verbal expression and enhanced descriptions of the children". In a few cases there were elements of a child-centered approach, when the children made unexpected arguments as to how they recognized someone ("it's Yiorgos, I smell him, because he's my friend"). The main focus of children's interest seemed to be on the form of the subject (the appearance and aesthetic characteristics of the parts of the body), with which the children were engaged ("I had a hard time because Stephanos has the same hair as Tito", "Miss, it's unfair, it's harder to understand with the palms"). It seemed the children experienced this tactile game as a means to teach the subject and during the activity they used "many adjectives and modifiers in referring to parts of the body".

The children who took part in activity E3 (Dialogues) seemed to interact under internal conditions of learning, expressing personal views and feelings (dialogue between the two hands of one child whose mother was pregnant: "Will you be a good baby? –Yes"). A diary entry confirms this observation: "When they presented the dialogue, many children had intense expressions on their faces". For most children the activity was a learner-centered situation in which "anything having to do with the content or meaning of the works of the children was up to them" (dialogues between two hands: "How heavy this bag is! –Come, let's do it together", "Many children talked about morning dialogues with their parents in which they spoke about the stress school causes them and their unwillingness to go"). Rarely, the children displayed an informative approach ("Miss, how can they have a dialogue since hands can't talk?"). The kind of focus that was apparent in the activity had to do with feelings and the meanings the children attributed to the subject. It was frequently observed that the children's comments contained personifications, imaginary elements and were frequently influenced by their lives ("it's lucky there are two of us so we can hear better", "it speaks that way because it doesn't have friends"). All of this is demonstrated by the fact that both the children's works and their comments were original and diverse. It is also worth noting that many children displayed signs of creatively approaching the subject, e.g. it was observed that "with their words and movement of their body parts, some children created original and humorous situations on purpose". The theatricality of this activity made most children feel that they were participating in a drama lesson. Children attributed aesthetic/expressive traits to parts of the body and focused on the way the parts of the body "spoke" ("introducing one leg to another", dialogue between two index fingers: "You're naughty and can't have a party. No, I'll be good"). Of note was that two children in the sample diagnosed with high-functioning autism responded to the demands of this activity.

In activity P3 (Restrictions) the children's experience seemed more related to external environmental conditions in terms of the taught subject. Nevertheless it was not rare to see these conditions combined with emotions and personal meanings (without all limbs "I couldn't fight the bad guys"). Although the children in this activity seemed almost exclusively to use informational and technical elements with regard to the subject ("They repeatedly tried to do the movement they were instructed to do", "I broke my arm and in the summer I couldn't swim in the sea"), there were quite a few cases in which they combined interpretative/personal/transformative elements in the process ("There are people who don't have arms and I've seen them swim, I saw it on TV", "I would say bravo to them!"). The exercise was considered to combine the characteristics of the teacher- and learner-centered approach, providing children with mixed opportunities. Connecting the human body with life was the children's main focus. In quite a few cases they talked about the usefulness of the subject and the different ways each part of the body participates in social situations ("you crossed yourself with your hands", "he presses his foot on the gas pedal", "the head thinks", "with our lips we give kisses", "I can use one hand to say hello, like this [laughing] and to give a *mountza* [a traditional gesture of insult in Greece, spreading the fingers of one hand and pointing the palm at the person to be insulted], like this", "In the Olympic games they play basketball sitting in wheelchairs and get lots of points". "I know a man who doesn't have one hand and he jet skis and he got married!"). The artistic

Table 4.3 Positive indications (>50% of the sample) during the aesthetics-based teaching of "the human body"

ACTIVITIES	DATA ANALYSIS CRITERIA									
	Learning conditions involved		Teaching approaches		Focus on				Educational roles of art	
	external	internal	teacher-centered	learning-centered	the subject	the meaning	the form	the social pluralism/context	teaching object	teaching medium
R3 The movements of the subject	✓		✓		✓					✓
F3 Recognizing by touch	✓		✓				✓			✓
E3 Dialogues		✓		✓		✓			✓	
P3 Restrictions	✓	✓	✓	✓		✓		✓		✓

elements (music and motion) were used by most children as a teaching medium, to recall their social and personal experiences with the parts of their body ("with one hand you can't hug mommy tightly", "Makis is pushing me with his hands").

The types of behavior observed in over 50% of the sample during the implementations of the aesthetics-based activities integrated in the teaching of "the human body" are presented in Table 4.3.

4.5.4 Aesthetics-based teaching of "botany-flowers" (Natural Environment Studies Syllabus)

a. Description of the aesthetics-based teaching of "botany-flowers"

The activities designed to be integrated in the aesthetics-based teaching of "botany-flowers" are as follows:

R.4. PHYSICAL RENDERING OF THE SUBJECT

The educator reads a text having to do with the taught subject (flowers):

A small seed in the earth opens and from inside springs a short stem. Slowly, it grows and peeks up from the earth. The heat and light embrace it and a blossom appears. Every day the sun caresses the stem, it grows ever taller, while the blossom opens slowly. It opens up and becomes a flower that knows how beautiful it is. Now the flower is thirsty. A wind blows; it blows stronger and the flower is frightened. Fortunately the wind grows weaker and it begins to rain. The flower gets wet, but is no longer thirsty. Time passes, and the rain becomes a drizzle and stops. Evening comes, and the flower closes its petals to rest. In the morning, everything is calm. Suddenly, a bee sits on it and takes some pollen. It tickles. If it did not have roots, the flower would play chase with the bee or it would dance. But it doesn't matter, it will dance in place.

After a first reading, the text is read a second time while the children listen scattered around the classroom, with eyes closed. They render with their bodies what they listened to. In the following discussion, the children refer to various parts of the text, and the movements they made to represent it. The theoretical foundation of the activity is **representationalist**.

E.4. IN OUR IMAGINATION

The children are then called upon to create "a flower they like very much, but could only exist in their imagination". At their disposal are materials to paint, make collages or sculptures. Each child then presents his/her work and explains their ideas. The theoretical foundation of the activity is **expressionist/cognitivist**.

F.4. ART GALLERY

With the teacher's help, the children group the works made in the previous activity, having set various morphological criteria (e.g. based on the material used, or the color of the paper in the background or other aesthetic choices) and place each group in a different corner of the classroom. The classroom turns into an art gallery. The children exit the classroom and enter quietly, acting like visitors to an art exhibition. They observe "how the flowers are made in each work", for example, they look at the size, colors, how much space in the paper was used etc. They then discuss their observations, and comparisons of the works. The theoretical foundation of the activity is **formalist**.

P.4. POSSIBLE OCCURRENCES

In the last stage of this program, each child presents a brief theatrical scene of an event or possible event in their lives, in which the taught subject (flowers) plays a main part. After each presentation, a discussion follows connected to what children know or have experienced in terms of the role of flowers in their lives, in what context they place flowers in their lives, and their views on them in each case. The theoretical foundation of the activity is **postmodernist/contextualist**.

b.   Results of the aesthetics-based teaching of
   "botany-flowers"

The aesthetics-based teaching of "botany-flowers" came from implementations of the preceding activities, which were implemented in kindergarten classes, in this order: R4 (Physical rendering of the subject), E4 (In our imagination), F4 (Art gallery), P4 (Possible occurrences). The same order is followed in presenting the results.

   In activity R4 (Physical rendering of the subject) the children seemed to base their experience mainly on external learning conditions, influenced by the content of the text the teacher read. Indicative comments were: "The children represented parts of the text and situations with similar bodily shapes", and "In the discussion they wanted to show the shapes they had made and comment on whether they looked like flowers, spontaneously recalling their knowledge on the subject" ("I made petals with my fingers", "this is how I made the leaves on the stem", "I turned my face to the sun"). It is interesting that in one group, there was a discussion about the "proper" movements to represent a flower. The discussion concluded that "the movements are similar, but not identical", because "we're all representing different flowers". There were some cases in which the children added internal conditions, filling in content that was not in the text ("when it rained, lightning struck, and burnt me", "they proposed making scenery and laid down fabric on the ground to look like dirt") or ascribing emotional elements to the text ("They were concerned that the flower was scared, and they asked me what I was doing to protect it"). The children seemed to feel they were participating in a teacher-centered approach that had an informational orientation (Generalist teacher: "Bravo children, you made similar movements and it looked like a choreography"). During the discussion, the children asked the teacher questions for clarification such as, "Miss, do flowers grow every day?". Also indicative was a repeated observation that "The generalist teachers considered the activity effective because it seemed that the children were learning and repeated what they had been taught about the development of a flower", "The children referred to many flowers and frequently exchanged information on them". There were a few instances indicating a child-centered approach of the subject ("I was a giant flower"). Children's focus was mainly on the subject of flowers. This is demonstrated by their frequent comments about knowledge they had on the subject ("I've seen bees and they sit on the flower and take the pollen and tickle it", "I've seen it in my grandma's garden"). Some comments showed a trend by fewer children to utilize this activity for self-expression (dialogue between two children: "Lambros, don't hurry to get up, go slower. –I'm growing faster than the other flowers"). Physical expression was used as a teaching medium ("They used their trunks to represent the stem of the flower, spread their arms to represent the leaves, or posed them is such a way so that they represented buds and petals", "the teacher praised the children because they looked like flowers"). It was also observed that, "In their comments, the children repeated the terminology of botany (petals, stem, root, bud etc.)".

Activity E4 (In our imagination) seemed to be an opportunity for the children to utilize internal interactions between themselves and the subject. Characteristically, the instructions they were given were "you can make a flower however you imagine it being, . . . however you like . . . it might exist nowhere but in your imagination". The children's interest was almost exclusively centered on attributing meaning and emotion to the taught subject. Indication of this was the fact that "the works were diverse and contained many original elements" such as "a flower that has a rainbow that is only white and yellow", "a chocolate flower", "a ballerina flower and we dance together", "a flower that lives in the sea", "a flower that grew up in a junkyard". Generally, it was observed that in the activity, the children connected the works of art with the creator frequently using possessives ("mine", "Yiannis' flower"). It is worth noting that many children's flowers had special abilities, were resilient, or had the characteristics of heroes who help humanity solve its problems. Their engagement with art (creating and responding to visual art works) seemed to be very much like an art class because the children focused on the aesthetic elements of the subject and were left to express themselves on the subject ("the leaves become wings and it flies and pours out lava", "it has eyes and sees everywhere and tells me about it"). In one group, indeed, there was a discussion about an individual's need to express themselves artistically: "There were objections to the unrealistic elements in some works" ("flowers don't fly!") and answers such as "we are drawing what we imagine, not what is", "imagination is different (in each person)".

In activity F4 (Art gallery), many children seemed to base their learning experience on external conditions ("let's put all the red ones together", "during the visit to the art gallery they talked in whispers and encouraged others to do so because 'that's what you do in galleries and museums'"). There were, however, quite a few cases when the children thought up internal and unexpected criteria for classifying the works: "they divided the works based on how many flowers there were in each painting, in pots (one flower), and gardens (many flowers)". Teaching frequently seemed to be teacher-centered and informational. The children asked technical/aesthetic questions such as "Should we put the drawings together that have things?" (about drawings with three-dimensional elements) and seemed "to learn to articulate judgments and the follow rules that apply in places where art is exhibited". It was also observed that frequently their teachers suggested manners of critiquing and organizing the works. Despite this, at times it seemed as if the children felt free to "express their own aesthetic criteria" and the teaching adopted a rather child-centered approach. The children's interest was almost exclusively drawn to the form of the taught subject and they functioned intellectually, judging the aesthetic qualities, comparing the materials and techniques used ("the colors are the same, almost, both of them, but I used colored pencils and Nefeli used magic markers", "we put them together because these have the same colors, they have the same as those", "I put mine with Eleni's because she also used blue glitter and drew with yellow and light blue and green, and they have the same beads"). Also, the children seemed to be trying to think in an abstract manner about their works ("Miss, you can't group them, they're all different!"). For almost all the children the activity seemed to be a situation of teaching arts (observing and critiquing visual arts works) and art was the taught object. Indicatively it was observed that the children frequently "looked at the flowers of the others with great interest and compared them with their own, in terms of shape, color, size and materials used" ("in this one, the petals are circles instead of curved lines", "all her flowers are big", "these don't have stems", "but how can paintings have a smell?", "it's not only my painting that's pretty, I like other ones too").

During activity P4 (Possible occurrences), it seemed the children were at times influenced by external conditions ("I cut flowers", "I put flowers and water in the vase", "I water", "She is planting", "He is selling") and at other times with internal conditions ("I show my mother love", without flowers "I'd be bored", "I would be sad"). The subject of the skits and the children's comments seemed to be guided by the teacher and had to do with the information the children had on the subject ("we have aloe at home and we use it when we hurt ourselves, my grandma hurt herself and used aloe and she got better", "she's putting on perfume", "she was holding a bouquet at her wedding"). Most children focused on comprehending the social structures in which the taught subject exists and functions (e.g. sex, nationality, sociopolitical conditions etc.). It was clear that the children were engaged recalling experiences and connecting them to what was being taught. The role of art (pantomime) was rather that of a teaching medium, both when the children used the pantomime as a mode to express the social dimension of flowers and their use in human life ("I made a wreath for May Day", "just like mommy, I put a flower behind my ear to be pretty"), as well as when they perceived the subject through an emotional filter ("they smell beautiful, they give honey and love" "(without flowers) the garden would be without colors", "terrible").

Table 4.4 presents the types of behavior that 50% of the children or above seemed to have adopted.

4.5.5 Aesthetics-based teaching of "water – the cycle of water" (Natural Environment Studies Syllabus)

a. Description of the aesthetics-based teaching of "water – the cycle of water"

The following experiential aesthetics-based activities were designed to be used in teaching "water – the cycle of water":

R.5. AUDIO REPRESENTATION

The children are called upon to mimic the sounds of various phenomena related to the taught subject. They work in small groups. Each group works

Table 4.4 Positive indications (>50% of the sample) during the aesthetics-based teaching of "botany-flowers"

ACTIVITIES	DATA ANALYSIS CRITERIA									
	Learning conditions involved		Teaching approaches		Focus on				Educational roles of art	
	external	internal	teacher-centered	learning-centered	the subject	the meaning	the form	the social pluralism/ context	teaching object	teaching medium
R4 Physical rendering of the subject	✓		✓		✓					✓
E4 In our imagination		✓		✓		✓			✓	
F4 Art gallery	✓	✓	✓	✓			✓		✓	
P4 Possible occurrences	✓	✓	✓					✓		✓

to prepare its own audio composition, and then presents it to the rest of the class which listens with eyes closed. The class is asked to name the subject of the work, that is, the phenomenon presented in it. In the end, all the children are called to order the works according to the "cycle of water". The theoretical foundation of the activity is **representationalist**.

F.5. WORKS OF ART ON THE SUBJECT

With the help of the educator and their parents, the children are asked to seek out works of art (paintings, songs, stories) which contain the element of water. They can search on the internet, in the school library, their own homes or anywhere else. Some of the works are presented and provide the basis for discussion on the forms and manners in which the cycle of water is represented. Children learn about different works and their creators and are asked to express their views and taste. The theoretical foundation of the activity is **formalist**.

E.5. ADVENTURES OF THE SUBJECT

The children then work in small groups and organize a theatrical event depicting the "adventures of a drop of water". They present their skit to the group and comment upon it. The theoretical foundation of the activity is **expressionist/cognitivist**.

P.5. POSITIVE AND NEGATIVE

Finally, the educator holds a discussion with the children about the positive and negative experiences people can have with water. The children are asked to draw whatever it is that most impressed them in the discussion. The works are then presented and classified into two groups: positive and negative experiences with water. The theoretical foundation of the activity is **postmodernist/contextualist**.

b.   Results of the aesthetics-based teaching of
"water – the cycle of water"

To examine the aesthetics-based teaching of "water – the cycle of water" the preceding activities were implemented in kindergarten classes, in this order: R5 (Acoustic representation), F5 (Works of art on the subject), E5 (Adventures of the subject) and P5 (Positive and negative). The results are presented in the same order.

Activity R5 (Acoustic representation) seemed for almost all the children a chance to interact with external conditions having to do with the taught subject. The children mimicked sounds such as "sea and storm", "drizzle", "running brook", "storm". Most of the children's comments, both during the preparation to compose their work ("that doesn't look like a wave", "let's put drops that do this") and during the discussion on each work ("I was confused by this sound"), were indications of an informational teaching approach. The children assigned to the teacher the role of the person who has knowledge on the subject ("the children asked a lot of questions about the sounds of the phenomena, about their order etc."). The subject itself seemed to be the focus of interest ("first let's put in the rain and then the sea", "this is the sound the snow makes [pause], isn't so, Miss, it doesn't have a sound?"), but there were quite a few signs that interest was focused on the form of the sounds ("it was a big river, is that why it was so loud?"). Art (creating and playing an audio work) functioned as a means of teaching the subject. In other words, during the activity the children referred to natural phenomena related to the cycle of water ("they talked about their knowledge on the phenomena and their order", "in communicating with the teacher and among themselves, there were many references to and exchanges of knowledge about the subject").

In Activity F5 (Works of art on the subject) children brought internal conditions to perceive the subject. They chose works of art and were interested in the way these affected themselves and the creators of the works. In other words, the children approached the variety that can exist when different people, in different ages and using different arts can shape thoughts and feelings about water ("all artists like the sea just like I do", "it looks more like rain in this painting). The teaching approach was at times teacher-centered and informational ("he lived a long time in the past?") and at times child-centered ("the children chose the works they liked and analyzed the meanings they gave them"). In fact, it was observed that different art forms influenced the teaching in different ways ("in teaching a song, the children frequently seemed to be concerned with identifying facts about water in the lyrics, while during a discussion about the stories they referred more to the feelings the subject elicited"). The form of the taught subject in every work was the focus of interest for the children. Many children seemed to perceive the various arts as modes of communication and as different aspects of significant forms ("I listen to the song and it seems to me that I'm listening to the sea", "the artist went into the picture, just like Mary Poppins", "I prefer this painting. I like it that the river is gray"). The children seemed to consider their artistic engagement as an arts class, as their comments were mainly about "the different characteristics of each art", "frequently compared the aesthetic traits of the taught subject in every work" and "many questions had to do with the lives of the artists". In a particular group of the sample a discussion arose about the meaning of artists being "inspired" by natural phenomena.

In activity E5 (Adventures of the subject) internal factors of learning were activated almost exclusively ("they identified with the drop", "expressed feelings about what was the matter with it"). The teaching approach seemed for most children to be child-centered ("they enhanced their knowledge on the subject with personal, imaginary elements"). Children seemed to feel free to express their personal views on the subject and determine the development and results of the activity ("Teacher: 'Is something the matter?' Student: 'Yes, the drop, when it rained, it flew high like a transparent bird and didn't fall to the ground. It was scared that cars and heavy lorries might run it over"). All of the children were focused on producing their own meanings on the subject. In their stories they portrayed ideas the taught subject had elicited ("I'm happy and so light, the wind can waft me around", "The drop stuck on to an angry cloud and was scared, and cried, it didn't like everyone arguing. It wanted to go to the lake", "It carried a sword and sat on the cloud like it was a horse"). Children behaved as if they were participating in an arts lesson (creating a skit and performing). They seemed to be preoccupied with the aesthetic elements of the lesson and gave the taught subject a symbolic dimension. Indicatively, "in their skit, two children pretended the drop was swimming happily in the sea and sang the song they had learned in the previous activity (Thalassa plateia [Wide sea] Manos Hatzidakis, 1970)". However, many children's stories seemed to be influenced by what they had learned about water and the natural phenomena. This was considered to be an indication that for these children the activity functioned as teaching through the arts.

During activity P5 (Positive and negative) many of the children relied on external conditions of perceiving the subject. However, they frequently expressed their beliefs on the taught subject according to their internal factors of perception ("I'm afraid to swim. Last summer I almost drowned in the sea"). The children's experience of the teaching approach also seemed to be mixed. They were guided by the teacher with regard to the cognitive, realistic environment related to the taught subject, and seemed to experience an informational teaching situation ("do you all know what a flood is?", "there were discussions about drought in other parts of the world"). When called upon to classify the phenomena they had been taught about into positive and negative experiences, the children seemed to interpret the knowledge they had and in some cases to transform their views of the subject ("I've drawn the well we have in the garden, which I love. It has a blue bucket, there it is. Let's put it in the good list! —Yes, it will be Nikos' good well"). Both through their comments and their drawings it was clear their focal point was the variety of manifestations of water ("Children considered positive their experiences from drinking water, swimming, washing clothes,

Table 4.5 Positive indications (>50% of the sample) during aesthetics-based teaching of "water – the cycle of water"

ACTIVITIES	DATA ANALYSIS CRITERIA									
	Learning conditions involved		Teaching approaches		Focus on				Educational roles of art	
	external	internal	teacher-centered	learning-centered	the subject	the meaning	the form	the social pluralism/ context	teaching object	teaching medium
R5 Acoustic representation	✓		✓		✓		✓			✓
F5 Works of art on the subject		✓	✓	✓			✓		✓	
E5 Adventures of the subject		✓		✓		✓			✓	✓
P5 Positive and negative	✓	✓	✓	✓				✓		✓

watering the garden, washing their teeth, cleaning the house etc., while the negative experiences were catching cold because it rained, floods, drought, storms – ships sinking"). Art (painting and analyzing-classifying works) was considered more as a teaching medium in correlating the taught subject with human experience. This was made clear during the analysis of their works of art when they were mainly occupied with the content of every experience depicted. For a few children, the activity was an opportunity simply to engage in creating art ("A child spent a long time trying to render in her drawing the feeling of thirst").

In Table 4.5. are the results of the aesthetics-based activities incorporated into the lesson on "water – the cycle of water". The table contains the types of behavior observed in 50% of participants and above.

4.5.6 Aesthetics-based teaching of "surrealism" (Visual Arts Syllabus)

a. *Description of the aesthetics-based teaching of "surrealism"*

The activities designed to be used in teaching "surrealism" are as follows:

F.6. REPRODUCTION

A copy of Joan Miró's *The Harlequin's Carnival* is presented to the class.

(**Joan Miro, Carnaval d'Arlequin** (Carnival of Harlequin), 1924–1925. Oil on canvas, support: 26 × 36 5/8 inches [66.04 × 93.0275 cm]; framed: 36 3/4 × 47 × 3 1/8 inches [93.34 × 119.38 × 7.94 cm]. Collection Albright-Knox Art Gallery, Buffalo, New York; Room of Contemporary Art Fund, 1940 [RCA1940:8]. © Successió Miró S.L./Artists Rights Society (ARS), New York/ADAGP, Paris https://www.albrightknox.org/artworks/rca19408-carnaval-darlequin-carnival-harlequin).

The children are asked to look at it, then choose a small part of the painting to draw so that it looks as much as possible like the original in terms of shape, color and size. Upon finishing, one child places his/her painting on a surface and the remaining children place their own works following the composition of the original painting. A place in the painting is sought for each child's drawing and they are compared with the original. The theoretical foundation of the activity is **formalist**.

R.6. DEFINING THE SUBJECT

A discussion takes place about "the curious, unreal" things in the painting. The children are asked to represent some of them with their bodies. The educator keeps notes of what the children are saying and photographs their static representations. Thus, a verbal and bodily definition of "surrealism" ensues. Based on this, the educator reveals the term to them, and provides them with relevant information. The theoretical foundation of the activity is **representationalist**.

E.6. SOUNDTRACK

The educator discusses with the children the meanings they ascribe to the painting, asking especially about its various parts. Then he/she asks, "what kind of sounds would be heard from this part of the painting?" The children make up a sound or brief audio motif. The process is repeated for various parts of the painting. The children's suggestions as to the sounds are rendered with voices, body sounds and instruments (e.g. Orff-Schulwerk instruments). The teacher points to parts of the painting and the children produce the respective sounds. The entire work is recorded. Upon listening to it, improvements can be made (e.g. in terms of the order of the sounds), if the children suggest it. The final work is played and commented on as musical background to the "surrealistic painting". The theoretical foundation of the activity is **expressionist/cognitivist**.

P.6. PERSONAL EXPERIENCES

A child is called upon to tell the group about something he/she has experienced frequently, but which they regard as "strange", that seems more "imaginary" than real, that is, something that he/she perceives as "surreal". The entire group then decides how the child's story can be dramatized in a brief skit. This process is repeated for every child who wishes to share their "surrealistic" thoughts and experiences with the group. In the following discussion, they analyze how such experiences affect their life. The theoretical foundation of the activity is **postmodernist/contextualist**.

b.   Results of the aesthetics-based teaching of "surrealism"
     (Visual Arts Syllabus)

Results from the aesthetics-based teaching of "surrealism" came from the implementations in first grade classes of the following activities in this order: F6 (Reproduction), R6 (Defining the subject), E6 (Soundtrack) and P6 (Personal experiences).

   In activity F6 (Reproduction) most children seemed to be activated in terms of the external conditions of learning, using the painting as a model to mimic the taught subject. All the children seemed to experience a direct, teacher-centered, informational teaching method in which the accuracy of the reproduction of the painting was their main goal ("Miss, it [the painting] should have been a bit bigger, isn't that right?", "How do I do it?" "I'm trying to make that color that's like fire", "you should put the dice up high, above the stars"). Most children's comments also showed their focus on the forms of elements in the painting ("What shape is it? Like a square", "it's night because the sky is dark through the window", "many colors", "'I see these intense colors", "the guitar is very small, smaller than I made it", "I made this hand without a body, it's long and like a hose"). In this activity, the children seemed to benefit from practicing the techniques, acquiring knowledge and making judgments on the structural characteristics of the painting related to the taught subject ("The blue is the same everywhere, on the table and the window, and the cone in the butterfly", "Yes, which magic marker do you use? I think with this crayon"). The activity functioned as a teaching art class for most children who seemed to benefit on an aesthetic level. Indications of this was that "many arts materials were used", "the children used aesthetic terminology related to the painted elements", "All the children named many of the materials and used technical vocabulary", "they talked about the painting's structure, its distinct elements and their composition" ("The wheel is above the moustache", "This black triangle striking. No, more striking is the green sphere", "It has lots of small things, you see more, and more, and more", "curves and straight, many-colored").

In activity R6 (Defining the subject), the children experienced external conditions and isolated the elements in the painting "that could not be realistic", to describe in bodily movements ("I've got my tongue out and I'm doing this with my hands to represent one of the two fairies flying up there, the one with the huge tongue", "What are you? –That strange cat"). The children seemed to be experiencing rather direct, informational teaching, in which they chose to represent samples of the surrealist thought of painter ("it's one eye by itself", "I've never seen that before", "There is a butterfly with a red tongue. –It's fire, not a tongue"). All children seemed to focus on the subject of the painting ("the cat's moustache is wandering aaaaall over the room, like this", "I'm pretending to be an ear that is walking up the stairs", "they're fairies, not elves", "he put a guitar on top of the crinkly cone"), to define the subject being taught ("they tried to repeat the taught term 'surrealism' and it was not easy; they tried again syllable by syllable") and to reach conclusions such as, "It was in his mind, Miró's", "in a dream", "it's strange". In the discussion, children's focus on the subject was evident from the questions they asked requesting more information ("are there others like it? [paintings]", "why is its name so hard a name [surrealism]?"). Fewer children seemed to focus on the structure and form of the painting ("it's hard to draw, he must have been drawing for 40 hours"). Even fewer children seemed to focus on the meaning of the painting and the artist's emotions ("why did he paint that?", "was he happy or sad?"). For most children their engagement with art (representation through movement) functioned as a teaching medium and a means to understand the taught subject. They seemed to process the information derived from movement and finally define the subject and memorize the term ("they said the word, syllable by syllable", "it's strange", "we do it when we're confused", "it's in the imagination"). Some children seemed to benefit on an aesthetic level, using the activity rather as an art class and connecting their knowledge of works of art ("at the museum there are other paintings like this where things are mixed up").

During activity E6 (Soundtrack) it seemed the learning process was influenced by internal conditions for most children in the sample ("The sounds should be scary because the painting scares me. –No, they should be happy, sound like when all of us laugh out loud"). All of the children experienced this activity as child-centered. An indication of this was the fact that the development of the activity was determined by the children's ideas and decisions, as the educators reported that "the children proposed sounds", "chose what sounds they would include in their work, the sequence, how many sounds". Furthermore, during the entire process the children seemed to acoustically interpret, and in some cases transform, their views on the taught subject. In fact, quite a few children expressed positive conclusions about surrealism, such as that it was "a way to say strange things", "it's like a secret code". It was observed that most children were focused mainly on the feelings and meanings they ascribed to the surrealist painting, and more generally to surrealism ("budrdrdr, let's put that kind of sound, because the painting is like gibberish"). The children seemed to be trying to render in sound the emotions and effect the painting had on them. At times they tried to detect the meaning of the painting by looking back to the painter's (Miró) biography ("Was he blind?", "Did he have a mother?"). It is also worth noting the children frequently suggested sounds with formalistic arguments such as: "it has to be a long sound, like the black hand that is flying". The children seemed to regard the artistic process (composing an acoustic work) as a way to aesthetically approach the taught subject. There were comments that the situation had a dual nature, that is, it combined teaching through art (engaging in a subject with art as a tool) ("the children seemed to understand the concept being taught better") with teaching art ("the children engaged in artistic processes based on the taught subject").

The activity P6 (Personal experiences) was considered to be a situation in which both external and internal learning conditions developed "both simultaneously and combined". Most of the children's comments had to do with the contexts which they believed favored surrealistic thought ("dreams and imagination"), and the meanings they attributed to these thoughts. The children seemed to regard the teaching as rather child-centered as, during the activity, they felt free to share their experiences ("dreams", "experiences in a plane", "rides at an amusement park") and analyzed the ways they interpret these experiences ("I was flying without fearing that I'd crash"). In their comments the children seemed to focus on the specific conditions that would lend themselves to the development of surrealistic thought ("every day at nap time I feel that I'm dancing, my eyes are closed", "my soul is up high in the dream", "with my brain I am in Albania [my country] with grandma, but I am not there", "in my imagination I can do everything"). Another focal point for the children's interest was the meanings they gave to the concept being taught ("it is something that is not real", "they could call it, it's called 'strangism'"). Children seemed mainly engaged in the aestheticity of the process (theatrical performance of surrealistic experiences). The child explaining his/her "surrealistic" experience took on the roles of the "creator of the skit and the director" of the performance that followed. This child frequently "gave instructions on the organization of the event, explaining the meanings he/she wanted to express". The process thus seemed to assign art the role of the taught object and seemed to be a class in the dramatic arts.

The results of the aesthetics-based teaching program of "surrealism" are presented in brief in Table 4.6. The table contains the types of behavior observed in 50% of participants and above.

4.6 Other results

The findings collected from the paragraphs in the diaries in the section called "other observations" are presented here. They do not correspond to the criteria for analysis adopted, but were, nevertheless, considered relevant to the purpose of the study and enlightening as to future research on the subject. All of the comments considered to be repeated constituted two basic categories. The first had to do with the metacognitive content of children's comments (Chatzipanteli, Grammatikopoulos, & Gregoriadis, 2014; Kurt & Kurt, 2017; Larkin & Flannery Quinn, 2015; Van de Kamp, Admiraal, Van Drie, & Rijlaarsdam, 2015), the second was children's comments indicating their spontaneous, intensive involvement and the vigorous communication among them (Csíkszentmihályi, 2014; Dailey & Hauschild-Mork, 2017; Garrett, 2013; Markovic, 2011; Miller, 2007; Pope, 2001; Rooney, 2004; Winner et al., 2013).

The comments on the metacognitive content that stood out were those reporting on the ways the children were thinking ("We can do this, too", "Some things I see, I like, but I don't feel anything", "–I always like mine

Table 4.6 Positive indications (>50% of the sample) during aesthetics-based teaching of "surrealism"

ACTIVITIES	DATA ANALYSIS CRITERIA									
	Learning conditions involved		Teaching approaches		Focus on				Educational roles of art	
	external	internal	teacher-centered	learning-centered	the subject	the meaning	the form	the social pluralism/context	teaching object	teaching medium
F6 Reproduction	✓		✓				✓		✓	
R6 Defining the subject	✓		✓		✓		✓		✓	✓
E6 Soundtrack		✓		✓		✓	✓		✓	✓
P6 Personal experiences		✓		✓		✓		✓	✓	

best of all –Because it's yours or because it's the best? –Probably because it's mine", "We can't do everything"). Also, in this category were included children's conclusions about the way they perceived the taught subject ("We do it when we're confused", "In a dream", "It happens in nature") and insights with a philosophical dimension ("Imagination is different [in everyone]", "When they're similar it's not easy to make classifications", "God made us with different parts of our bodies so that we're different", "It's not wrong to paint something that doesn't exist").

In addition, during the activities the children showed signs of spontaneous deep involvement in the process ("They were surprised when the time came for the next scheduled activity", "Perfect!", "Can we do it again?", "Shh! He's ruining the game"). Most children exhibited signs such as a creative response to the subject ("asking for feedback", "in the later hours they referred to the activity and exercises and asked for the activities to be repeated", "creating original works and critiquing them, much problem-solving, humorous behavior"). Also noteworthy is that most aesthetics-based activities seemed to create conditions in which children became socially active about the taught subject ("they interacted among themselves and with the teacher", "seemed willing to talk", "verbally shared their experiences"). There were repeated observations that they followed rules of a high level of communication ("when one child presented something, the rest listened carefully", "the educators frequently adopted behaviors such as rewording, an accepting stance, and active listening to the children explaining their works"). Also, frequently the generalist teachers noted a willingness to communicate in children "who were usually aloof in collective activities in the class", and among children who "were in a program of parallel support or an inclusion in the education program".

5 Discussion

The first issue that would be interesting to discuss is, if the activities examined as experiential aesthetics-based create a teaching environment commensurate with the theoretical basis on which they were designed. In the following section the evidence as to the effect all the activities had on the children will be examined in groups, classified as to their theoretical foundation (representationalist, expressionist/cognitivist, formalist or postmodernist/contextualist). The examination of the evidence is based on the most intense influences that each activity had on the children (those that were observable in 50% or more of the children), as these are considered to have determined the main characteristics of the teaching situation. It is necessary, however, to mention that in practice every activity presented other types of influence (in smaller percentages) that corresponded to the other theoretical foundations, creating interesting amalgams.

Thus, the discussion that follows arises from comparing the most frequent findings from implementing activities with a common design foundation, to see if the activities cause the children to have experiences with common characteristics. In discussing this topic, conclusions may arise as to the possibility that each approach of aesthetic theory can constitute the theoretical framework of a corresponding type of arts integration activities.

Yet another important issue that needs to be discussed is if the teaching situations that arise during the implementation of activities based on different theoretical underpinnings are complementary. In other words, there must be a discussion on whether there is pedagogical interest arising from the teaching situation created by the different aesthetic foundation activities as a whole. A discussion of this issue can lead to conclusions on whether it is necessary to implement combinations of multiple kinds of the experiential aesthetics-based arts integration activities in teaching the same subject.

5.1 Discussion on the findings of the representationalism-based activities

To examine the indications of how the activities designed based on the representationalist theoretical approach affected children's perceptions of the teaching experience, a comparison is made among the findings of activities R1, R2, R3, R4, R5 and R6. Table 5.1 contains a brief presentation of findings of these activities to facilitate the comparison.

Even a brief glance at Table 5.1. shows that in the representationalism-based activities, behaviors were observed that had common characteristics in line with the respective theoretical framework (Barrett, 2017; Cannatella, 2008; Eisner, 1992b, 1996; Fleming, 2012; Martin & Schwartz, 2014). More specifically, during all the representationalism-based activities, external conditions much more than internal ones were involved in the learning process. This was attributed to the fact that the children were called upon to use mimesis in these activities. In addition, in all of these activities most children experienced the teaching method used as having an informational slant, with teacher-centered characteristics (Bresler, 1992; Efland, 1990a; Herberholz & Hanson, 1995; Spidell-Rusher et al., 1992). During the activities children were encouraged to produce similar works and relatively homogeneous results (e.g. pantomime, descriptions, verbal and non-verbal articulation of definitions). In contrast, there were few observations about the children controlling developments or having opportunities to perceive the taught subjects in a metaphorical way, in any of the representationalism-based activities. Furthermore, most children seemed to focus mainly on the subject matter, and rarely on the form of the subject or its connection to human life. It seemed that through the representationalism-based activities children worked mainly on learning the subject and had opportunities to benefit from understanding and memorizing information on the subject (Barnes, 1987; Bresler, 1992; Efland, 1990a; Spidell-Rusher et al., 1992). In accordance with all this, the arts seemed to constitute a teaching medium for most children, that is, a means to approaching the realistic elements of the subject being taught (Baker, 2013; Bilhartz et al., 2000; Burnaford et al., 2007; Chapman, 2015; Goldsmith et al., 2016; LaJevic, 2013; Lindström, 2012; Luftig, 2000; Rabkin & Redmond, 2004; Robinson, 2011; Sotiropoulou-Zormpala, 2012b).

Table 5.1 Indications of the characteristics of children's learning experience in the representationalism-based activities

REPR.-BASED ACTIVITIES	Characteristics of the children's learning experience							Educational roles of art		
	Learning conditions involved		Teaching approaches		Focus on			the social pluralism/ context	teaching object/	teaching medium
	external	internal	teacher-centered	learning-centered	the subject	the meaning	the form			
R.1. Physically expressing words	✓	✓	✓		✓					✓
R.2. The teacher has amnesia	✓		✓		✓					✓
R.3. Movements of the subject	✓		✓		✓					✓
R.4. Physical rendering of the subject	✓		✓		✓					✓
R.5. Acoustic representation	✓		✓		✓		✓			✓
R.6. Defining the subject	✓		✓		✓		✓		✓	✓

Given that the representationalism-based activities trigger specific types of outcomes, one could say that they constitute a specific type of arts activities which could be called "representationalist".

5.2 Discussion on the findings of the expressionism/ cognitivism-based activities

In order to seek the common elements of the learning experience created by the expressionism/cognitivism-based activities, the results of activities E1, E2, E3, E4, E5 and E6 are compared. The results are presented in Table 5.2. The types of behavior that the majority of the children seemed to exhibit in the expressionism/cognitivism-based activities can be found for the most part in the same columns in Table 5.2; in their majority the behaviors were common and in fact corresponded to the respective philosophical and educational theoretical exemplars (Dewey, 1966; Efland, 2002; Herberholz & Hanson, 1995; Langer, 1953; Lowenfeld & Michael, 1982; Read, 1956; Rousseau, 1762/1921).

Internal learning conditions prevailed, and the children developed their own understanding related to the taught subject. The children's comments showed that they frequently identified with the subject and artworks related to it and were moved by these. It was also evident that in all the activities the children experienced the teaching method as child-centered and having a transformational orientation. They often displayed a willingness or need to share their thoughts on the taught subjects and/or the aesthetic stimuli related to them. The activities seemed to function as a space to feel emotions (empathy frequently, and mutual understanding) and produce meanings which were not provided for in the curriculum. The instructions for the activities had to do with the process the children had to follow but never determined the outcomes of their works, which differed from child to child and group to group (Burton, 2000; DeCarvalho, 1991; Dorn, 2000; Efland, 1990a, 1990b; Entwhistle, 1970; Henry, 2002; Herberholz & Hanson, 1995; Jeffers, 1999; Rasanen, 1997; Rogers, 1983). The children seemed to focus on the meanings which in their opinions the taught subject bore, that is to utilize the activities as opportunities to interpret the subject in personal and original ways and impart to it characteristics related to the way in which they perceive it. In this context they seemed to develop their interpretative abilities and expressive skills (verbal and non-verbal), and cultivate their creativity (originality, imagination, humor) with regard to what they are learning (Abbs, 1996; Bastos & Zimmerman, 2015; Copple & Bredeckamp, 2009; Dailey & Hauschild-Mork, 2017; Davey, 1989; Eisner, 2002; Lowenfeld & Michael, 1982; Vygotsky, 2004). There seemed to be frequent alternations in the manner children used the arts in these activities between

Table 5.2 Indications of the characteristics of children's learning experience in the expressionism/cognitivism-based activities

EXPR./COGN.-BASED ACTIVITIES	Characteristics of the children's learning experience									
	Learning conditions involved		Teaching approaches		Focus on				Educational roles of art	
	external	internal	teacher-centered	learning-centered	the subject	the meaning	the form	the social pluralism/context	teaching object	teaching medium
E.1. Creating a skit		✓		✓		✓			✓	✓
E.2. Characters of the subject		✓		✓		✓			✓	✓
E.3. Dialogues		✓		✓		✓			✓	
E.4. In our imagination		✓		✓		✓			✓	
E.5. Adventures of the subject		✓		✓		✓			✓	✓
E.6. Soundtrack		✓		✓		✓	✓		✓	✓

a teaching object and a teaching medium (Lindström, 2012), as well as instances in which the two were mixed (Sotiropoulou-Zormpala, 2012a, 2012b, 2016). This occurred because in the expressionism/cognitivism-based activities it seemed that denotation alternated with connotation of the taught subjects, or an in-between situation developed: serving but also transcending the contents of the curriculum, defining, but also redefining the taught subjects, learning and understanding, but also interpreting whatever the children are taught (White, 2009).

Based on the preceding, one could argue that the expressionism/cognitivism-based activities constitute a specific type of arts integration activities which could be called "expressionist/cognitivist".

5.3 Discussion on the findings of the formalism-based activities

In order to reveal the characteristics of the experiences the children had in participating in the formalism-based activities, the findings from activities F1, F2, F3, F4, F5 and F6, were compared, and are presented in Table 5.3.

The experiences of the children who participated in the formalism-based activities exhibit similar characteristics which, in fact, revealed the association of the activities with their theoretical basis (Broudy, 1987, 1994; Smith, 1991). It seemed the children were influenced primarily by external learning conditions of a cognitive and technical orientation (Efland, 1990b). Internal conditions influenced the children's learning to a lesser extent. They felt they were experiencing a rather informational teaching approach in which the development of the activities and the general specifications of their works were determined by the educators. In some aspects of the instructions, children were encouraged to act on their own initiative. All of these activities seemed to contribute to the children's aesthetic development, providing opportunities to practice their artistic skills, aesthetically approach the subject and criticize the subject in terms of its form (Anderson & McRorie, 1997; Barrett, 2017; Hobbs, 1993; Efland, 1990b, 2004a; Feldman, 1992; Freedman, 2003; Freedman & Stuhr, 2004; Hurwitz & Day, 2007; Smith, 2002). Most the children's comments revealed that they were using their senses, different ways of composing their works, comparing, classifying, prioritizing, responding and arguing on the subject and its form. It was indicative that during the formalism-based activities the children's comments seemed often to be characterized by the use of adjectival modifiers and aesthetic terms. There are indications that these activities contribute to aesthetic development. More specifically children developed criteria used to subject both the taught material and the artworks to aesthetic interpretation and judgment (Barrett, 2017; Smith, 2002). All of

Table 5.3 Indications of the characteristics of children's learning experience in the formalism-based activities

FORMALISM-BASED ACTIVITIES	Characteristics of the children's learning experience								Educational roles of art	
	Learning conditions involved		Teaching approaches		Focus on					
	external	internal	teacher-centered	learning-centered	the subject	the meaning	the form	the social pluralism/context	teaching object	teaching medium
F.1. Critique	✓		✓	✓			✓		✓	
F.2. Human sculptures	✓	✓	✓				✓		✓	✓
F.3. Recognizing by touch	✓		✓				✓			✓
F.4. Art gallery	✓	✓	✓	✓	✓		✓		✓	
F.5. Works of art on the subject		✓	✓	✓			✓		✓	
F.6. Reproduction	✓		✓				✓		✓	

the formalism-based activities seemed to create the conditions in which art was utilized as an aesthetic object (the children were called upon to process the form of the subjects and the artworks related to it) and to constitute a teaching art situation (Broudy, 1987, 1994; Efland, 1990b; Greer, 1984; Smith, 1989, 1991, 2002). In a few activities the arts also functioned simultaneously as a teaching medium, that is, while processing the form of the taught subject, the children seemed to understand its contents better (Gude, 2008, 2013; Sandell, 2009).

From the preceding one could conclude that formalism-based activities constitute a specific type of arts integration activities which could be called "formalist".

5.4 Discussion on the findings of the postmodernism/ contextualism-based activities

The experiences of the children participating in the postmodernism/contextualism-based activities are revealed in the findings of activities P1, P2, P3, P4, P5 and P6. The findings are presented in Table 5.4 so as to discuss them comparatively.

It is clear that, as in the other aesthetics-based activities, the experiences of the children participating in the postmodernism/contextualism-based activities had many common characteristics that were consistent with their theoretical foundations (Barrett, 2017; Butler, 2002; Efland, 2007; Hutchens & Suggs, 1997; Jameson, 1991; Shusterman, 2005). During the activities most of the sample was experiencing a situation in which the children were influenced by both external and internal learning conditions. This seems to be a natural consequence of the instructions given for the activities, according to which the children were called upon first to recall their experiences of and second to express their views on the taught subject. The teaching approach the children seemed to experience was mixed, that is, both their academic/cognitive and expressive/creative endeavors of the children were encouraged. Within this context, they seemed to approach information on the social dimension of the subject and to have opportunities to transform their views based on their personal criteria (Anderson et al., 2010; Anderson & McRorie, 1997; Duncum, 2000; Freedman, 2000). The teaching in these activities had teacher-centered periods in which the children referred to the connections between the subject and real life, and their thinking seemed to have an academic/cognitive orientation. At the same time the children frequently determined the developments of the activity, displaying metaphorical/interpretative thinking and critical speech in the form of questions. Also, during the activities the children's focus was mainly on connecting the subject to their experiences. Sometimes their focus was on the subject's

Table 5.4 Indications of the characteristics of children's learning experience in the postmodernism/contextualism-based activities

CONT./POSTMOD.-BASED ACTIVITIES	Characteristics of the children's learning experience								Educational roles of art	
	Learning conditions involved		Teaching approaches		Focus on					
	external	internal	teacher-centered	learning-centered	the subject	the meaning	the form	the social pluralism/context	teaching object	teaching medium
P.1. Visitors	✓	✓	✓	✓				✓	✓	✓
P.2. A world without …	✓		✓					✓		✓
P.3. Restrictions	✓	✓	✓	✓		✓		✓		✓
P.4. Possible occurrences	✓	✓	✓					✓		✓
P.5. Positive and negative	✓	✓	✓	✓				✓		✓
P.6. Personal experiences	✓	✓		✓		✓		✓	✓	

multiple versions, depending on the context in which it exists and functions (Anderson, 2003; Anderson & Milbrandt, 2005; Gude, 2008). Furthermore, the activities based on the postmodernist/contextualist aesthetic approaches seemed more frequently to function as situations of teaching the subject through the arts, thus imparting the role of a teaching medium to art. It seems possible that children can benefit mainly on a social level, as the subject in these activities is examined and judged with regard to the structures that have to do with human life (personal experiences, cultural elements, international structures, human values) (Anderson, 2003; Anderson & Milbrandt, 2005; Duncum, 2002a; Efland, 2004b; Freedman, 2000; Gude, 2008; Sandell, 2009).

The preceding discussion reveals that the postmodernism/contextualism-based activities constitute a specific type of arts integration activities that could be called "postmodernist/contextualist".

5.5   Discussion on the combinations of the activities

An overview of the findings of the different types of aesthetics-based activities (Tables 5.1, 5.2, 5.3 and 5.4) sheds light on the nature of the entire learning experience of the children participating in the programs consisting of representationalist, expressionist/cognitivist, formalist and postmodernist/contextualist activities.

Looking at the totality of the implementations, it seems that using activities with a different theoretical framework in teaching the same subject gives rise to situations in which the children perceive the objective, social and cultural conditions related to the subjects taught. On the other hand subjective, internal, psychological conditions influence their perceptions of the subjects. The first situation was observed mainly during the representationalist and formalist activities, and the second situation was observed more in the expressionist/cognitivist activities, whereas in the postmodernist/contextualist activities there seemed to be an opportunity for synergy of the two situations. The indication that the children had opportunities to utilize both external and internal learning conditions was considered to be a positive element in the proposed strategy, in line with current scholarship on learning theories which consider this necessary (Brinkema, 2014; Davydov, 1990; Dislen, 2013; Heron, 1992, 2009; Hetland et al., 2013; Illeris, 2009; Jarvis, 2006; Lave, 2009; Wenger, 1998; Ziehe, 2009).

The instances in which the children seemed to experience a direct, teacher-centered, informational teaching situation were equal to those in which children considered the teaching as indirect, child-centered and transformational. In the representationalist, formalist and postmodernist/contextualist activities the majority of the students responded to the educator's specifications, reproduced information they had been taught, and their works exhibited homogeneity to an extent. In other words, in this type of activity they adopted behaviors suitable for a teacher-centered approach (Adams & Engelmann, 1996). In the expressionist/cognitivist activities the overwhelming majority of the children seemed to behave autonomously and/or independently, to have a sense of control over their actions, therefore indicating that they felt they were in a child-centered situation (McCombs & Whisler, 1997; Wright, 2006). This seemed also to be the case frequently in the postmodernismt/contextualist activities and the formalist activities.

It seems therefore that combining implementations of experiential aesthetic-based activities with different theoretical underpinnings might contribute to varied teaching situations. In this way, the prospect arises of creating a balanced teaching approach, which addresses, on the one hand, the imparting of information, and, on the other hand, a qualitative and transformational processing of this information. Contemporary research has noted the significance of the synergy of the two teaching methods, teacher- and learner-centered (Rimm-Kaufman et al., 2005; Zevin, 2000), and the respective learning experiences, informational and transformational (Borich, 2007; Burden & Byrd, 2010; Epstein, 2007; Kegan, 2009; Mello, 2007; Mezirow, 2009; Omrod, 2014; Orlich et al., 2007). At the foundations of contemporary theories of learning is the belief that "transformational kinds of learning need to be more clearly distinguished from informational kinds of learning, and each needs to be recognized as valuable in any learning activity, discipline, or field" (Kegan, 2009, p. 42). Furthermore, educators today seem to support combinations of these two seemingly opposite teaching methods (Goldstein, 2008; O.E.C.D., 2006; Tafa, 2011).

Every type of the aesthetics-based activities seemed to correspond to a different kind of the children's focus of interest in the subject they were being taught. During the representationalist activities the children seemed to focus primarily on the taught subject (Barnes, 1987; Bresler, 1992; Cannatella, 2008; Eisner, 1992b, 1996; Fleming, 2012; Spidell-Rusher et al., 1992); in the expressionist/cognitivist activities children focused on the feelings and meanings ascribed to the subject (Abbs, 1996; Burton, 2000; Davey, 1989; Dewey, 1966; Dorn, 2000; Eisner, 1992b, 1996; Henry, 2002; Jeffers, 1999; Martin & Schwartz, 2014; Rasanen, 1997); in the formalist activities the children seemed to be focused mainly on the form of the subject (Anderson & McRorie, 1997; Bell, 1913/1958; Broudy, 1987, 1994; Carroll, 1999; Fried, 1998; Greenberg, 1961, 1982; Feldman, 1992; Smith, 1991; Walton, 1970; Zangwill, 2001); and in the postmodernist/contextualist activities they seemed to look at multiple versions of the subject, depending on the context in which it was perceived (Anderson, 1997; Dorn, 2005; Duncum, 2001, 2002b, 2009; Efland, 2007; Elkjaer, 2009; Freedman, 2003; Jameson, 1991; Pearse, 1997; Shusterman, 2005; Tavin, 2005; Tavin & Hausman, 2004). The implementations indicated that the programs comprising the four examined types of experiential aesthetics-based activities constitute a strategy on which a multifaceted and multifocusing arts integration, as is described in the literature (Anderson & McRorie, 1997; Barrett, 2017; D' Olimpio & Teachers, 2016; Efland, 1990b; Hetland et al., 2013; Sandell, 2009; Van Leeuwen, 2015), can be built.

In the different types of aesthetics-based activities the children seemed to ascribe to the arts at times the role of a teaching object, and at others the role of a medium of the teaching process (Burnaford et al., 2007; Bresler, 2007; Eisner, 1999, 2002; Gelineau, 2012; Goldberg, 2012; Griffin et al., 2017; Luftig, 2000; Rabkin & Redmond, 2004; Robinson, 2011; Russell & Zembylas, 2007). In other words, the children seemed to feel that at times they were being taught the arts, and at others they were being taught a subject through the arts. In fewer, but in quite a few implementations, the majority of the children seemed to experience a mixed situation. The formalist activities were teaching arts situations in which the children were mainly preoccupied with aesthetic process. Most children who took part in the representationalist and postmodernist/ contextualist activities seemed to experience a situation of being taught a subject through the arts and the arts were used as a tool for teaching the subject. From their participation in the expressionist/cognitivist activities most children seemed to experience a mixed situation, that is, they were occupied in aesthetic processes, but ones which were related to the taught subject. In other words, they used the arts to approach the taught subject aesthetically. Each of the two roles ascribed to the arts when they are integrated into education yields significant, yet different, benefits discussed in the literature (Anderson, 2016; Argyriadi & Sotiropoulou-Zormpala, 2017; Baker, 2013; Chapman, 2015; Denac, 2014; Hetland et al., 2013; Ho, 2016; Goldsmith et al., 2016; LaJevic, 2013; Lilliedahl, 2018; Narey, 2008; Nathan, 2014; Scripp et al., 2013; Webster & Wolfe, 2013; Winner et al., 2013). The potential of the experiential aesthetics-based activities to be alternated and thus merge the benefits underlines the importance of this strategy. The fusion of these two roles opens up prospects for the cognitive element to be complemented by the aesthetic and vice versa, as it should be in aesthetic teaching (Granger, 2006; Macintyre-Latta, 2004; Pike, 2004; Sotiropoulou-Zormpala, 2012b, 2016).

The synopsis of the discussion on the entirety of the findings are in Table 5.5.

Table 5.5 Most frequently observed types of behavior identified during the aesthetics-based activities

CRITERIA OF ANALYZING DATA	AESTHETICS-BASED ACTIVITIES			
	Representationalist activities	*Expressionist/ cognitivist activities*	*Formalist activities*	*Postmodernist-contextualist activities*
Learning conditions involved	External conditions	Internal conditions	External conditions	External & internal conditions
Teaching approaches	Teacher-centered, direct, informational	Child-centered, indirect, transformational	Teacher-centered, direct, informational	Teacher-centered, direct, informational
Focus on/ Engagement	The subject/Managing information	The meanings/ Expressing emotions and meanings	The form/Mastering art knowledge and techniques	Social pluralism/Connecting to social structures
Educational roles of art/Arts integration as	Teaching medium/ Teaching through the arts	Mixed role	Teaching object/ Teaching arts	Teaching medium/Teaching through the arts

6   Conclusions and proposals

This book examines the possibility for aesthetic theory to be used as the basis for designing and implementing arts activities suitable for integration in school curricula in preschool and primary education. The implementations that took place shed light on the pedagogical benefits of such activities that, based on their general and specific characteristics, could be called *experiential aesthetics-based arts integration activities*. It is necessary to clarify that the teaching proposal introduced in this book is not a method whose steps need to be implemented precisely, nor is it a recipe proposed to reveal the ingredients of arts integration. What is being proposed is a map of actions that the designers and implementers of arts education can follow, aiming at isolated goals or weaving a fabric of goals, or both, with flexibility.

According to the indications that arose, experiential aesthetics-based activities designed on the same theoretical underpinnings influence pupils' learning experiences in a similar way. It seems possible that the aesthetic theoretical approach used as a basis to design the arts integration activities affects the children's experiences with regard to the kind of conditions they involve in the learning process; with regard to the type of teaching situation the children believe they are participating in; with regard to their focus of interest on the subject they are being taught; and with regard to the way in which they use the arts. Briefly, it was determined that every theoretical aesthetic approach (representationalism, expressionism/cognitivism, formalism and postmodernism/contextualism) can inspire the design of arts integration activities and influence corresponding teaching environments. Each of the aesthetic approaches, functioning as a different way of encountering the taught subjects and the aesthetic works related to them, encourages a different type of experience, and therefore creates prospects for different pedagogical outcomes.

A multifaceted and balanced teaching may develop from combining the four types of aesthetic-based activities. Combining the representationalist, expressionist/cognitivist, formalist and postmodernist/contextualist activities allows for a significant range of learning conditions, teaching methods, children's focus of interest, and ways of using the arts. More specifically, if the four types of experiential aesthetics-based activities are used in combination, it is likely that children may exploit situations in which external and internal learning conditions alternate or are merged. As a result, children can interact on the one hand with the denotative, conventional, objective and literal dimension of taught subjects, and on the other hand with their connotative, subjective and metaphorical/interpretative dimension. Furthermore, participating in a program consisting of the proposed variety of aesthetics-based activities, children may benefit both from direct, teacher-centered, informational teaching of a subject, and from an indirect, child-centered, transformational approach. That is, the teaching includes conveying information on a subject and the artworks related to it, but also opportunities for the children to feel free to approach the subject creatively and to redefine it. Thus, it may be possible to create a balance between serving the aims of the curriculum and transcending them. Moreover, in combining the four types of experiential aesthetics-based activities children have opportunities to focus on multiple facets of the taught subject and reap multiple learning benefits. With this strategy, it is possible for children to approach the content of a subject, develop the feelings and meanings it gives rise to, analyze its form and comprehend its different versions depending on the context in which they perceive it. These types of emphasis can lead to four types of aesthetic knowing close to those articulated by Reimer (1992): "I know what", "I know why", "I know how" and "I know through". By integrating the four different types of activities in teaching the same subject, children can utilize both the intrinsic and the instrumental benefits that engagement with art can offer them. Thus, art provides opportunities both to develop on an aesthetic level and more generally to grow personally and academically (Upitis, 2011). In terms used to describe the educational role of the arts, the proposed aesthetics-based design includes both *teaching art* and *teaching through the arts*. These two situations seem to appear at times by turns and at times in combination, to coexist and/or merge, thus creating the conditions for a high level of incorporating the arts into the teaching process that could be called *aesthetic teaching*.

From this, it seems clear that a conscious or unconscious preference for a particular aesthetic approach as a theoretical basis for arts education in school can lead to pedagogical bias. For example, in a design based exclusively on the representationalist approach, the respective arts activities offer children opportunities to be influenced by external/social learning conditions, to participate in an informational, teacher-centered situation, to focus mainly on the subject taught and to use the arts they engage in mainly as a teaching medium (first column of Table 5.5). This teaching will not be holistic or balanced. It will deprive students of the benefits that seemed to arise in the expressionist/cognitivist, formalist, or postmodernist/contextualist approach to taught subjects, which can be different (even contradictory) and function in a complementary and/or merged way. This complementary way of using the different aesthetic approaches could increase the fulfillment of the learning experience for children.

The experiential aesthetics-based arts integration activities as a whole can contribute to "purging" teaching of certain problematic tendencies that are prevalent in contemporary education. It was observed that the programs of the activities provided the children with opportunities to break free of the strictly cognitive goals on the taught subject (learning a given, objective and quantitatively evaluated piece of knowledge); to avoid reproducing whatever they were taught exclusively following the models of behaviorism; to allow their desire to enter into the process of learning; to criticize, think creatively, express subjective ideas; to be productive; to innovate. In addition, participating in the programs of the activities the children seemed to complement their intellectual activation using other elements of their natural endowments such as bodily, emotional and social abilities. According to yet another general observation, the experiential aesthetics-based arts integration activities seemed to give children plenty of opportunities to avoid the verbalism that usually prevails in classrooms and to use sounds, colors, shapes, textures, motions, expressions etc. as alternatives to words and to include a variety of modes of meaning-making and communication in the learning process.

This study demonstrates a functional manner of connecting the various views of aesthetic theory with the design and implementation of aesthetic teaching. The detailed description of the implementations, as well as the fact that the evidence was extracted from the reactions of the children themselves, are factors that help make comprehensible important elements of the teaching situation that develops in experiential aesthetics-based arts integration activities. Nevertheless, the undertaking of this study is an initial exploration of a proposal worth examining in greater depth and scope. In order to produce generalizable results on the subject of the study, further research is needed using a larger and randomly selected sample, with interventions of longer duration. In addition, it is important to examine issues such as the combination of various types of learning styles with activities of a particular aesthetic foundation, the metacognitive dimensions of aesthetics-based activities and their contribution to developing learning motivation and deep engagement of the children in the teaching processes. Furthermore, it would be a good direction if future research were to turn to the significance of hybrid, synergistic activities that could arise from combining different aesthetic approaches. Also worthy of examining are issues related to the education of in-service and pre-service teachers, so that they can successfully design and implement experiential aesthetics-based activities.

For now it could be said that the field of aesthetic approaches is capable of providing a structured theoretical basis for arts integration in teaching and guiding the manner in which respective practices can be designed and implemented in kindergarten and primary school. The different approaches to analyzing art and the aesthetic experience may be used as channels to permeate teaching processes with aestheticity. The endeavor is not simple but not so complex as to be unmanageable by the generalist or art teacher. It is also a challenging endeavor because it creates situations in which children's experiences in school can be varied, multifaceted, multimodal and holistic. This is demonstrated by the varied, imaginative and spontaneous meanings, full of pleasure, surprise and humor, expressed by the children who participated in the experiential aesthetic-based arts integration activities. Their comments still echo in our ears: "I put my two ears to talk together, but they had nothing to say. But my two hands had a lot to talk about. Listen: . . .", "I like the other kids' paintings, not only my own", "everyone has a different imagination", "this is what the snow sounds like (pause)", "How do you draw thirst?", "Did Miró have a mother?"

References

Abbs, P. (1996). The new paradigm in British arts education. *Journal of Aesthetic Education, 30*(1), 63–71.

Abell, K. (2006). Realism and the riddle of style. *Contemporary Aesthetics, 4*, 376.

Adams, G. L., & Engelmann, S. (1996). *Research on direct instruction: 25 years beyond DISTAR.* Seattle, WA: Educational Assessment Systems.

Aguirre, I. (2004). Beyond the understanding of visual culture: A pragmatic approach to aesthetic education. *Journal of Art Craft and Design, 23*(3), 256–269.

Allison, B., & Hausman, J. (1998). The limits of theory in art education. *Journal of Art & Design Education, 17*(2), 121–127.

Alperson, P. (1991). What should one expect from a philosophy of music education? *Journal of Aesthetic Education, 25*(3), 215–242.

Anderson, E. (2016). Learning from an artistically crafted moment: Valuing aesthetic experience in the student teacher's drama education. *International Journal of Education & the Arts, 17*(1). Retrieved from www.ijea.org/v17n1/

Anderson, T. (1997). Toward a postmodern approach to art education. In J. Hutchens & M. Suggs (Eds.), *Art education: Content and practice in a postmodern era* (pp. 62–73). Reston, VA: National Art Education Association.

Anderson, T. (2003). Art education for life. *The International Journal of Art & Design Education, 22*(1), 58–66.

Anderson, T., Gussak, D., Hallmark, K., & Paul, A. (Eds.). (2010). *Art education for social justice.* Reston, VA: National Art Education Association.

Anderson, T., & McRorie, S. (1997). A role for aesthetics in centering the K-12 art curriculum. *Art Education, 50*(3), 6–14.

Anderson, T., & Milbrandt, M. K. (2005). *Art for life: Authentic instruction in art.* Boston, MA: McGraw-Hill.

Argyriadi, A., & Sotiropoulou-Zormpala, M. (2017). Engaging first-graders in language arts through "arts-flow activities". *Curriculum Perspectives, 37*(1), 25–38.

Aristotle. (1995). *Poetics (together with Longinus, on the Sublime & Demetrius, on style).* (D. Halliwell, Trans.). Loeb Classical Library Vol. 199. Cambridge, MA: Harvard University Press.

Attwood, A. I. (2015). *Aesthetic literacy through the avant-garde: Establishing an aesthetically responsive curriculum.* Doctoral dissertation. Washington

State University, 3715154. Retrieved from https://pqdtopen.proquest.com/doc/1710106661.html?FMT=AI

Baker, D. (2013). Art integration and cognitive development. *Journal for Learning Through the Arts, 9*(1).

Barnes, R. (1987). *Teaching art to young children.* London: Unwin Hyman.

Barrett, T. (1997). Modernism and postmodernism: An overview with art examples. In J. Hutchens & M. Suggs (Eds.), *Content and practice in a postmodern era.* Reston, VA: The National Art Education Association.

Barrett, T. (2017). *Why is that art? Aesthetics and criticism of contemporary art* (3rd ed.). New York, NY and Oxford: Oxford University Press.

Bastos, F., & Zimmerman, E. (Eds.). (2015). *Connecting creativity research and practice in art education.* Reston, VA: National Art Education Association.

Beardsley, M. (1981). *Aesthetics: Problems in the philosophy of criticism* (2nd ed.). Indianapolis, IN: Hackett Publishing Company, Inc.

Bell, C. (1958). *Art.* New York, NY: Capricorn Books (Original work published 1913).

Bilhartz, T. D., Bruhn, R. A., & Olson, J. E. (2000). The effect of early music training on child cognitive development. *Journal of Applied Developmental Psychology, 20*, 615–636. doi:10.1016/S0193-3973(99)00033-7

Blocker, G. (1979). *Philosophy of art education.* New York, NY: Charles Scribner's Sons.

Blumenfeld-Jones, D. S. (2012). *Curriculum and the aesthetic life: Hermeneutics, body, democracy, and ethics in curriculum theory and practice.* New York, NY: Peter Lang.

Booyeun, L. (2004). Aesthetic discourses in early childhood settings: Dewey, Steiner, and Vygotsky. *Early Child Development and Care, 174*(5), 473–486.

Borich, G. D. (2007). *Effective teaching methods: Research-based practice.* Upper Saddle River, NJ: Pearson Merrill/Prentice Hall.

Bresler, L. (1992). Visual art in primary grades: A portrait and analysis. *Early Childhood Research Quarterly, 7*(3), 397–414.

Bresler, L. (2002). Out of the trenches: The joys (and risks) of cross-disciplinary collaborations. *Council of Research in Music Education, 152*, 17–39.

Bresler, L. (Ed.). (2007). *International handbook of research in arts education.* Dordrecht, The Netherlands: Springer.

Brinkema, E. (2014). *The forms of the affects.* Durham, NC and London: Duke University Press.

Broudy, H. S. (1987). *The role of imagery in learning.* Occasional Paper 1. The Getty Centre for Education in the Arts.

Broudy, H. S. (1994). *Enlightened cherishing: An essay on aesthetic education.* Urbana, IL and Chicago, IL: University of Illinois Press.

Brouillette, L. (2010). How the arts help children to create healthy social scripts: Exploring the perceptions of elementary teachers. *Arts Education Policy Review, 111*(1), 16–24.

Brown, D. J. (2006). *Teachers implicit theories of expression in visual arts education: A study of western Australian teachers.* Ph.D. dissertation. Edith Cowan University. Retrieved from http://ro.ecu.edu.au/theses/52

Bruner, J. (1977). *The process of education.* Cambridge, MA: Harvard University Press. (Original work published 1960)

Burden, P. R., & Byrd, D. M. (2010). *Methods for effective teaching: Meeting the needs of all students* (6th ed.). Upper Saddle River, NJ: Pearson Education.

Burnaford, G., Brown, S., Doherty, J., & McLaughlin, H. J. (2007). *Arts integration frameworks, research and practice: A literature review.* Washington, DC: Arts Education Partnership.

Burton, J. M. (2000). The configuration of meaning: Learner-centered art education revisited. *Studies in Art Education, 41*(4), 330–339.

Butler, C. (2002). *Postmodernism: A very short introduction.* New York, NY: Oxford University Press.

Cannatella, H. (2008). *The richness of art education.* Rotterdam, The Netherlands: Sense Publishers.

Carroll, N. (1999). *Philosophy of art: A contemporary introduction.* London and New York, NY: Routledge.

Carroll, N. (2001). *Beyond aesthetics.* Cambridge, MA: Cambridge University Press.

Catterall, J. S. (2002). The arts and the transfer of learning. In R. J. Deasy (Ed.), *Critical links: Learning in the arts and student academic and social development* (pp. 151–157). Washington, DC: Arts Education Partnership.

Cazden, C. (2005). The value of conversations for language development and reading comprehension. *Literacy Teaching and Learning, 9*(1), 1–6.

Chapman, L. H. (1982). *Instant art instant culture: The unspoken policy for American schools.* New York, NY: Teachers College, Columbia University.

Chapman, S. (2015). Arts immersion: Using the arts as a language across the primary school curriculum. *Australian Journal of Teacher Education, 40*(9), 86–101.

Charlton, W. (2016). *Aesthetics: An introduction.* London and New York, NY: Routledge.

Chatzipanteli, A., Grammatikopoulos, V., & Gregoriadis, A. (2014). Development and evaluation of metacognition in early childhood education. *Early Child Development and Care, 184*(8), 1223–1232.

The College Board. (2013). *International standards for arts education: A review of standards, practices, and expectations in thirteen countries and regions.* Retrieved from www.nationalartsstandards.org/sites/default/files/College%20Board%20Research%20-%20International%20Standards_0.pdf

Collingwood, R. G. (1958). *The principles of art.* London, Oxford, and New York, NY: Oxford University Press.

Collins, A., Joseph, D., & Bielaczyc, K. (2004). Design research: Theoretical and methodological issues. *The Journal for the Learning Sciences, 13*(1), 15–42.

Constantino, T., & White, B. (2010). *Essays on aesthetic education for the 21st century.* Rotterdam, The Netherlands: Sense Publishers.

Cope, B., & Kalantzis, M. (Eds.). (2015). *A pedagogy of multiliteracies: Learning by design.* London: Palgrave.

Copple, C., & Bredeckamp, S. (Eds.). (2009). *Developmentally appropriate practice in early childhood programs serving children from birth through age 8.* Washington, DC: National Association for the Education of Young Children.

Cornett, C. (2011). *Creating meaning through literature and the arts: Arts integration for classroom teachers* (4th ed.). Boston, MA: Pearson.

Croce, B. (1995). *Aesthetic as science of expression and general linguistic* (D. Ainslie, Trans.). New York, NY: Routledge (Original work published 1902).

Csíkszentmihályi, M. (2014). *Applications of flow in human development and education: The collected works of Mihaly Csíkszentmihályi*. Dordrecht: Springer.

Dailey, R., & Hauschild-Mork, M. (2017). Making it all count: A cross-disciplinary collaboration model incorporating scholarship, creative activity, and student engagement. *InSight: A Journal of Scholarly Teaching, 12*, 64–78.

Danto, A. (1981). *The transfiguration of the commonplace*. Cambridge, MA: Harvard University Press.

Danto, A. (1992). *Beyond the brillo box: The visual arts in post-historical perspective*. New York, NY: Farrar, Strauss, and Giroux.

Davey, E. (1989). The cognitive in aesthetic activity. *Journal of Aesthetic Education, 23*(2), 107–112.

Davydov, V. V. (1990). *Types of generalization in instruction: Logical and psychological problems in the structuring of school curricula*. Reston, VA: National Council of Teachers of Mathematics.

Deasy, R. (Ed.). (2002). *Critical links: Learning in the arts and student academic and social development*. Washington, DC: Arts Education Partnership.

Deasy, R. (2003). *Creating quality integrated and interdisciplinary arts programs: A report of the arts education national forum*. Washington, DC: Arts Education Partnership.

DeCarvalho, R. J. (1991). The humanistic paradigm in education. *The Humanistic Psychologist, 19*(1), 88–104. doi:10.1080/08873267.1991.9986754

Denac, O. (2014). The significance and role of aesthetic education in schooling. *Creative Education, 5*, 1714–1719.

Dewey, J. (1934). *Art as experience*. New York, NY: Minton, Balch & Company.

Dewey, J. (1966). My pedagogic creed. In W. Baskin (Ed.), *Classics in education* (pp. 177–188). London: Vision Press.

Dickie, G. (1979). *Aesthetics: An introduction*. Indianapolis, IN: Pegasus.

Dislen, G. (2013). The reasons of lack of motivation from the students' and teachers' voice. *The Journal of Academic Social Science, 1*(1), 35–45.

D'Olimpio, L., & Teachers, C. (2016). Philosophy for children meets the art of living: A holistic approach to an education for life. *Philosophical Inquiry in Education, 23*(2), 114–124.

Dorn, C. M. (2000). The renewal of excellence. *Arts Education Policy Review, 101*(30), 17–18.

Dorn, C. M. (2005). The end of art in education. *Art Education, 58*(6), 47–54.

Dowling, C. (n.d.). Aesthetic formalism. In *Internet encyclopedia of philosophy*. Retrieved from www.iep.utm.edu/aes-form/#H3

Duncum, P. (2000). How art education can contribute to the globalisation of culture. *Journal of Art and Design Education, 19*(2), 170–180.

Duncum, P. (2001). Visual culture: Developments, definitions, and directions for art education. *Studies in Art Education, 42*(2), 101–112.

Duncum, P. (2002a). Theorising everyday aesthetic experience with contemporary visual culture. *Visual Arts Research, 28*(2), 4–15.

Duncum, P. (2002b). Clarifying visual culture. *Art Education, 55*(3), 6–11.

Duncum, P. (2009). Visual culture in art education. *Visual Arts Research, 35*(1), 64–75.

Eaton, M. (1988). *Basic issues in aesthetics*. Belmont: Wadsworth.

Efland, A. D. (1990a). *A history of art education: Intellectual and social currents in teaching the visual arts*. New York, NY: Teachers College Press.

Efland, A. D. (1990b). Art education in the twentieth century. In D. Soucy & M. A. Stankiewicz (Eds.), *Framing the past: Essays in art education* (pp. 216–236). Reston, VA: The National Art Education Association.

Efland, A. D. (2002). *Art and cognition: Integrating the visual arts in the curriculum*. New York, NY: Teachers College Press.

Efland, A. D. (2004a). Emerging visions of art education. In E. W. Eisner & M. D. Day (Eds.), *Handbook of research and policy in art education national art* (pp. 691–700). Mahwah, NJ: Lawrence Erlbaum Associates, Inc. Publishers.

Efland, A. D. (2004b). The entwining nature of the aesthetic: A discourse of visual culture. *Studies in Art Education, 45*(3), 234–251.

Efland, A. D. (2007). Arts education, the aesthetic and cultural studies. In L. Bresler (Ed.), *International handbook of research in arts education* (pp. 47–54). Dordrecht, NL: Springer.

Eisner, E. W. (1972). *Educating artistic vision*. New York, NY: Macmillan.

Eisner, E. W. (1976). *The arts, human development and education*. Berkeley, CA: McCutchan Publishing Corporation.

Eisner, E. W. (1992a). Aesthetic education. In *Encyclopedia of educational research* (Vol. 1, pp. 39–42). New York, NY: Macmillan.

Eisner, E. W. (1992b). Curriculum ideologies. In P. W. Jackson (Ed.), *Handbook of research curriculum* (pp. 302–326). New York, NY: Macmillan.

Eisner, E. W. (1996). *Cognition and curriculum reconsidered*. London: Paul Chapman Publishing Ltd.

Eisner, E. W. (1999). Does experience in the arts boost academic achievement? *Clearing House, 72*(3), 143–149.

Eisner, E. W. (2002). *The arts and the creation of mind*. New Haven, CT: Yale University Press.

Elkjaer, B. (2000). The continuity of action and thinking in learning: Re-visiting John Dewey. *Outlines: Critical Social Studies, 2*, 85–101.

Elkjaer, B. (2009). Pragmatism: A learning theory for the future. In K. Illeris (Ed.), *Contemporary theories of learning: Learning theorists . . . in their own words* (pp. 74–89). London and New York, NY: Routledge.

Emerson, R. M., Fretz, R. I., & Shaw, L. L. (2001). Participant observation and fieldnotes. In P. Atkinson, A. Coffey, S. Delamont, J. Lofland, & L. Lofland (Eds.), *Handbook of ethnography* (pp. 356–357). Thousand Oaks, CA: Sage.

Entwhistle, H. (1970). *Child-centred education*. London: Methuen.

Epstein, A. S. (2007). *The intentional teacher: Choosing the best strategies for young children's learning*. Washington, DC: National Association for the Education of Young Children.

Eurydice. (2009). *Arts and cultural education at school in Europe.* Brussels. Retrieved from http://eacea.ec.europa.eu/education/eurydice/documents/thematic_reports/113EN.pdf

Feldman, E. B. (1992). Formalism and its discontents. *Studies in Art Education, 33*(2), 122–126.

Fleming, M. (2012). *The arts in education: An introduction to aesthetics, theory and pedagogy.* London and New York, NY: Routledge.

Fleming, M., Bresler, L., & O'Toole, J. (2015). *Routledge international handbook of the arts and education.* London: Routledge.

Flewitt, R. (2013). Multimodal perspectives on early childhood literacies. In J. Larson & J. Marsh (Eds.), *The Sage handbook of early childhood literacy* (pp. 295–309). London: Sage.

Freedman, K. (2000). Social perspectives on art education in the U.S: Teaching visual culture in a democracy. *Studies in Art Education, 41*(4), 314–326.

Freedman, K. (2003). *Teaching visual culture: Curriculum, aesthetics, and the social life of art.* New York, NY: Teachers College Press.

Freedman, K., & Stuhr, P. (2004). Curriculum change for the 21st century: Visual culture in art education. In E. W. Eisner & M. D. Day (Eds.), *Handbook of research and policy in art education national art* (pp. 815–827). Mahwah, NJ: Lawrence Erlbaum Associates, Inc. Publishers.

Freeland, C. (2001). *But is it art? An introduction to art theory.* Oxford and New York, NY: Oxford University Press Inc.

Fried, M. (1998). *Art and objecthood: Essays and reviews.* Chicago, IL and London: University of Chicago Press.

Fry, R. (1920). *Vision and design.* London: Chatto and Windus Ltd.

Gandini, L., Hill, L., Cadwell, L., & Schwall, C. (2005). *In the spirit of the studio: Learning from the atelier of Reggio Emilia.* New York, NY: Teachers College Press.

Gardner, H. (2009). Multiple approaches to understanding. In K. Illeris (Ed.), *Contemporary theories of learning: Learning theorists . . . in their own words* (pp. 106–115). London and New York, NY: Routledge.

Garrett, C. E. (2013). Promoting student engagement and creativity by infusing art across the curriculum: The arts integration initiative at Oklahoma City University. *About Campus, 18*(2), 27–32.

Gee, J. P. (2004). *Situated language and learning: A critique of traditional schooling.* London: Routledge.

Gelineau, R. P. (2012). *Integrating the arts across the elementary school curriculum* (2nd ed.). Belmont, CA: Wadsworth Cengage.

Goldberg, M. (2012). *Arts integration: Teaching subject matter through the arts in multicultural settings.* Boston, MA: Pearson/Allyn and Bacon.

Goldsmith, L., Hetland, L., Hoyle, C., & Winner, E. (2016). Visual-spatial thinking in geometry and the visual arts. *Psychology of Aesthetics, Creativity and the Arts, 10*(1), 56–71.

Goldstein, L. S. (2008). Teaching the standards in developmentally appropriate practice: Strategies for incorporating the sociopolitical dimension of DAP in early childhood teaching. *Early Childhood Education Journal, 36,* 253–260.

Gombrich, E. H. (2000). *Art and illusion: A study in the psychology of pictorial representation* (Millennium, Ed.). Princeton, NJ and Oxford: Princeton University Press.

Goodman, N. (1976). *Languages of art: An approach to a theory of symbols* (2nd ed.). Indianapolis, IN: Hackett Publishing Company.

Goodman, N. (1978). *Ways of worldmaking.* Indianapolis, IN and Cambridge, MA: Hackett Publishing Company.

Goodman, N., Perkins, D., & Gardner, H. (1972). *Basic abilities required for understanding and creation in the arts: Final report.* Cambridge, MA: Harvard University, Graduate School of Education. Project no. 9-0283.

Gormley, K., & McDermott, P. (2016). The exclusion of the creative arts from contracted school curricula for teaching the common core standards. *Journal for Learning Through the Arts, 12*(1), 1–12.

Granger, D. (2006). Teaching aesthetics and aesthetic teaching: Toward a Deweyan perspective. *Journal of Aesthetic Education, 40*(2), 45–66.

Greenberg, C. (1961). *Art and culture.* Boston, MA: Beacon Press.

Greenberg, C. (1982). Modernist painting. In F. Frascina & C. Harrison (Eds.), *Modern art and modernism: A critical anthology* (pp. 5–10). London: Harper & Row and Open University Press.

Greene, M. (2001). *Variations on a blue guitar, the Lincoln center institute lectures on aesthetic education.* New York, NY: Teachers College Press.

Greer, W. D. (1984). Discipline-Based Art Education: Approaching Art as a Subject of Study. *Studies in Art Education, 25*(4), 212–218.

Griffin, S. M., Rowsell, J., Winters, K.-L., Vietgen, P., McLauchlan, D., &. McQueen-Fuentes, G. (2017). A reason to respond: Finding agency through the arts. *International Journal of Education and the Arts, 18*(25), 1–24.

Gude, O. (2004). Postmodern principles: In search of a 21st century art education. *Art Education, 57*(1), 6–14.

Gude, O. (2008). Aesthetics making meaning. *Studies in Art Education, 50*(1), 98–103.

Gude, O. (2013). New school art styles: The project of art education. *Art Education, 66*(1), 6–15.

Habermas, J. (1981). Modernity versus postmodernity. *New German Critique, 22*, 3–14.

Hagaman, S. (1990). Philosophical aesthetics in the art class: A look toward implementation. *Art Education, 43*(4), 22–39.

Hardiman, M., Rinne, L., & Yarmolinskaya, J. (2014). The effects of arts integration on long-term retention of academic content. *Mind, Brain, and Education, 8*(3), 144–148. doi:10.1111/mbe.12053

Hawkins, B. (2002). Children's drawing, self-expression, identity and the imagination. *Journal of Art and Design Education, 22*(3), 209–219.

Hellenic Pedagogical Institute–Hellenic Ministry of Education and Religious Affairs. (2003). Ministerial Decisions 21072a/C2 and 21072b/C2. *Cross-curricular thematic framework and curricula of primary and secondary education* [available in Greek]. Official Government Gazette 303 v. A' and 304 v. B'. Athens: National Printing Office.

Henry, C. (2002). Reflections on Manuel Barkan's contributions to art education. *Art Education, 55*(6), 6–11.

Herberholz, B., & Hanson, L. (1995). *Early childhood art* (5th ed.). Dubuque, IA: Brown.

Heron, J. (1992). *Feeling and personhood: Psychology in another key.* London: Sage.

Heron, J. (2009). Life cycles and learning cycles. In K. Illeris (Ed.), *Contemporary theories of learning: Learning theorists . . . in their own words* (pp. 129–146). London and New York, NY: Routledge.

Hesterman, S. (2013). Early childhood designs for multiliteracies learning. *Australian Journal of Language and Literacy, 36*(3), 158–168.

Hetland, L., Winner, E., Veenema, S., & Sheridan, K. (2013). *Studio thinking 2: The real benefits of visual arts education* (2nd ed.). New York, NY: Teachers College Press.

Hetland, L. & Winner, E. (2000). The arts and academic achievement: What the evidence shows. *Journal of Aesthetic Education, 34*(3/4), 3–10.

Ho, C. (2016). In search of an aesthetic pathway: Young children's encounters with drama. *Early Child Development and Care, 187*(1), 1–12.

Hobbs, J. A. (1993). In defense of a theory of art for art education. *Studies in Art Education, 34*(2), 102–113.

Hobbs, J. A. (1997). The interaction between art education and theories of art. In J. Hutchens & M. Suggs (Eds.), *Content and practice in a postmodern era* (pp. 47–61). Reston, VA: The National Art Education Association.

Hospers, J. (1969). The concept of artistic expression. In J. Hospers (Ed.), *Introductory readings in aesthetics* (pp. 142–167). New York, NY: Macmillan.

Hurwitz, A., & Day, M. (2007). *Children and their art: Methods for the elementary school* (8th ed.). Belmont, CA: Thomson Wadsworth.

Hutchens, J., & Suggs, M. (Eds.). (1997). *Art education: Content and practice in a postmodern era.* Reston, VA: National Art Education Association.

Illeris, K. (2009). A comprehensive understanding of human learning. In K. Illeris (Ed.), *Contemporary theories of learning: Learning theorists . . . in their own words* (pp. 7–20). London and New York, NY: Routledge.

jagodinski, J. (1991). A para-critical/sitical/sightical reading of Ralph Smith's excellence in art education. *Journal of Social Theory in Art Education, 11*, 119–159.

Jameson, F. (1991). *Postmodernism, or, the cultural logic of late capitalism.* Durham, NC: Duke University Press.

Jarvis, P. (2006). *Towards a comprehensive theory of human learning.* London: Routledge.

Jeffers, C. S. (1999). Lessons for art education from reading education: A commentary. *Studies in Art Education, 40*(3), 275–278.

Jewitt, C. (Ed.). (2009). *The Routledge handbook of multimodal analysis.* London: Routledge.

Jimenez, M. (1997). Qu'est-ce que l'esthétique ? Paris : Gallimard.

Kant, I. (2000). *Critique of the power of judgment* (P. Guyer & E. Matthews, Trans.). Cambridge, MA and New York, NY: Cambridge University Press (Original work published 1790).

Kegan, R. (2009). What "form" transforms? A constructive-developmental approach to transformative learning. In K. Illeris (Ed.), *Contemporary theories of learning: Learning theorists . . . in their own words* (pp. 35–52). London and New York, NY: Routledge.

Kieran, M. (2005). *Revealing art: Why art matters*. London: Routledge.

Kivy, P. (1997). *Philosophies of arts: An essay in differences*. Cambridge, MA: Cambridge University Press.

Kress, G. (2010). *Multimodality: A social semiotic approach to contemporary communication*. New York, NY: Routledge.

Krug, D. H., & Cohen-Evron, N. (2000). Curriculum integration positions and practices in art education. *Studies in Art Education, 41*(3), 258–275.

Kulvicki, J. (2006). *On images*. Oxford: Blackwell.

Kurt, M., & Kurt, S. (2017). Improving design understandings and skills through enhanced metacognition: Reflective design journals. *International Journal of Art & Design Education, 36*(2), 226–238.

LaJevic, L. (2013). Arts integration: What is really happening in the elementary classroom? *Journal for Learning Through the Art, 8*(1). Retrieved from http://files.eric.ed.gov/fulltext/EJ1018332.pdf

Langer, S. (1953). *Feeling and form: A theory of art*. New York, NY: Charles Scribner's Sons.

Larkin, S., & Flannery, Q. S. (2015). Metacognitive experiences: Taking account of feelings in early years education. In S. Robson (Ed.), *The Routledge international handbook of young children's thinking and understanding* (pp. 189–198). Abingdon: Routledge.

Lave, J. (2009). The practice of learning. In K. Illeris (Ed.), *Contemporary theories of learning: Learning theorists . . . in their own words* (pp. 200–208). London and New York, NY: Routledge.

Lilliedahl, J. (2018). Building knowledge through arts integration. *Pedagogies: An International Journal, 13*(2), 133–145.

Lindström, L. (2012). Aesthetic learning about, in, with and through the arts: A curriculum study. *International Journal of Art & Design Education, 31*(2), 166–179. doi:10.1111/j.1476-8070.2012.01737.x

Lopes, D. (1996). *Understanding pictures*. Oxford: Oxford University Press.

Lowenfeld, V., & Michael, J. A. (1982). *The Lowenfeld lectures: Viktor Lowenfeld on art education and therapy*. University Park, PA: The Pennsylvania State University Press.

Luftig, R. (2000). An investigation of an arts infusion program on creative thinking, academic achievement, affective functioning, and arts appreciation at three grade level. *Studies in Art Education, 41*(3), 208–227.

Lyotard, J.-F. (1984). *The postmodern condition: A report on knowledge* (G. Bennington & B. Massumi, Trans.). Minneapolis, MN: University of Minnesota Press.

Macintyre-Latta, M. (2004). Traces, patterns, textures: In search of aesthetic teaching/learning encounters. In D. M. Callejo-Perez, S. M. Fain, & J. J. Slater (Eds.), *Pedagogy of place* (pp. 79–96). New York, NY: Peter Lang.

Manzella, D. (1963). *Educationists and the evisceration of the visual arts*. Scranton, PA: International Textbook Company.

Markovic, S. (2011). Components of aesthetic experience: Aesthetic fascination, aesthetic appraisal, and aesthetic emotion. *I-Perception, 3*, 1–17. doi:10.1068/i0450aap

Martin, L., & Schwartz, D. L. (2014). A pragmatic perspective on visual representation and creative thinking. *Visual Studies, 29*(1), 80–93. doi:10.1080/14725 86X.2014.862997

McCombs, B. L., & Whisler, J. S. (1997). *The learner-centered classroom and school: Strategies for enhancing student motivation and achievement.* San Francisco, CA: Jossey-Bass.

Mello, R. (2007). Teaching for meaning-making and deep understanding in a general education theatre course. *Journal of the Scholarship of Teaching and Learning, 7*(2), 90–109.

Mezirow, J. (2009). An overview on transformative learning. In K. Illeris (Ed.), *Contemporary theories of learning: Learning theorists . . . in their own words* (pp. 90–105). London and New York, NY: Routledge.

Michaels, S., O'Connor, C., & Resnick, L. (2008). Deliberative discourse idealized and realized: Accountable talk in the classroom and in civic life. *Studies in Philosophy and Education, 27*, 283–297.

Miller, J. P. (2007). *The holistic curriculum.* Toronto: OISE Press.

Moore, R. (1998). History of aesthetic education. In *Encyclopedia of aesthetics* (2nd ed., pp. 89–93). New York, NY: Oxford University Press.

Morgan, D. (1988). *Focus group as qualitative research.* Thousand Oaks, CA: Sage.

Mouriki-Zervou, A. (2003). *Metamorphoses tis aisthitikis* [metamorphoses of aesthetics]. Athens: Nefeli.

Mouriki-Zervou, A. (2011). The cognitive dimension of art: Aesthetic and educational value. *The International Journal of Learning, 18*(1), 1–12.

Narey, M. (Ed.). (2008). *Making meaning: Constructing multimodal perspectives of language, literacy, and learning through arts-based early childhood education.* New York: Springer.

Nathan, L. (2014). Why arts? *The Educational Forum, 78*(4), 351–354. doi:10.108 0/00131725.2014.944075

The National Coalition for Core Art Standards. (2013). *The national core arts standards: A conceptual framework for arts learning.* Retrieved from http://nccas. wikispaces.com/

Neuendorf, K. (2002). *The content analysis guidebook.* Thousand Oaks, CA: Sage.

Newall, M. (2011). *What is a picture? Depiction, realism, abstraction.* New York, NY: Palgrave Macmillan.

Omrod, J. E. (2014). *Educational psychology: Developing learners* (8th ed.). Boston, MA: Pearson.

Organisation for Economic Co-operation and Development (O.E.C.D.). (2006). *Starting strong II.* Early childhood education and care. O.E.C.D.

Orlich, D. C., Harder, R. J., Callahan, R. C., Trevisan, M., Brown, A., & Miller, D. (2007). *Teaching strategies: A guide of effective instruction.* Boston, MA: Houghton Mifflin Company.

Parsons, M. J. (2004). Art and integrated curriculum. In E. W. Eisner & M. D. Day (Eds.), *Handbook of research and policy in art education* (pp. 775–794). Mahwah, NJ: Lawrence Erlbaum Associates.

Parsons, M. J., & Blocker, H. G. (1993). *Aesthetics and education*. Urbana, IL: University of Illinois Press.

Pearse, H. (1992). Beyond paradigms: Art education theory and practice in a post-paradigmatic world. *Studies in Art Education, 33*(4), 244–252.

Pearse, H. (1997). Doing otherwise: Art education praxis in a postparadigmatic world. In J. Hutchens & M. Suggs (Eds.), *Art education: Content and practice in a postmodern era* (pp. 31–39). Reston, VA: National Art Education Association.

Pike, M. (2004). Aesthetic teaching. *Journal of Aesthetic Education, 38*(2), 20–37.

Plato. (1974). *The republic* (D. Lee, Trans.). Harmondsworth: Penguin.

Pope, D. C. (2001). *Doing school: How we are creating a generation of stressed out, materialistic, and miseducated students*. New Haven, CT: Yale University Press.

Rabkin, N., & Redmond, R. (Eds.). (2004). *Putting the arts in the picture: Reframing education in the 21th century*. Chicago, IL: Columbia College Chicago.

Rasanen, M. (1997). *Building bridges, experiential art understanding: A work of art as a means of understanding and constructing self*. Helsinki: University of Art and Design Helsinki.

Read, H. (1956). *Education through art* (3rd ed.). London: Faber & Faber.

Reid, L. (1969). *Meaning in the arts*. London: George Allen & Unwin.

Reimer, B. (1992). What knowledge is of most worth? In B. Reimer & R. A. Smith (Eds.), *The arts, education and aesthetic knowing* (pp. 20–50). Chicago, IL: University of Chicago Press.

Richardson, D. (1992). *Teaching art, craft and design*. Melbourne: Longman Cheshire.

Rimm-Kaufman, S. E., La Paro, K. M., Downer, J. T., & Pianta, R. C. (2005). The contribution of classroom setting and quality of instruction to children's behavior in the kindergarten classroom. *Elementary School Journal, 105*(4), 377–394. doi:10.1086/429948

Robinson, A. (2011). Research review of the effects of arts integrated curriculum on student success. *International Journal of Arts and Sciences, 4*(11), 289–303.

Rogers, C. (1983). *Freedom to learn for the 80s*. Columbus, OH: Charles Merrill.

Rollins, M. (2001). Pictorial representation. In B. Gaut & D. Lopes (Eds.), *The Routledge companion to aesthetics* (pp. 297–312). London: Routledge.

Rooney, R. (2004). *Arts-based teaching and learning: Review of the literature*. Washington, DC: WESTAT Rockville, Maryland. Retrieved from www.kennedy-center.org/education/vsa/resources/VSAarts_Lit_Rev5–28.pdf

Rousseau, J.-J. (1921). *Emile, or education* (B. Foxley, Trans.). London and Toronto: J. M. Dent and Sons (Original work published 1762).

Russell, J., & Zembylas, M. (2007). Arts integration in the curriculum: A review of research and implications for teaching and learning. In L. Bresler (Ed.), *International handbook of research in arts education* (pp. 287–301). Dordrecht, The Netherlands: Springer.

Rymes, B. (2016). *Classroom discourse analysis: A tool for critical reflection* (2nd ed.). New York, NY: Routledge.

Sandell, R. (2009). Using form+theme+context (FTC) for rebalancing 21st-century art education. *Studies in Art Education, 50*(3), 287–299.

Scripp, L., Burnaford, G., Vazquez, O., Paradis, L., & Sienkiewicz, F. (2013). *Partnerships in arts integration research final reports.* Washington, DC: Arts Education Partnership.

Shusterman, R. (2005). Aesthetics and postmodernism. In J. Levinson (Ed.), *The Oxford handbook of aesthetics* (pp. 771–782). Oxford: Oxford University Press.

Smith, R. A. (Ed.). (1970). *Aesthetic concepts and education.* Urbana, IL: University of Illinois Press.

Smith, R. A. (1989). *Discipline-based art education.* Urbana, IL: University of Illinois Press.

Smith, R. A. (1991). Philosophy and theory of aesthetic education. In R. A. Smith & A. Simpson (Eds.), *Aesthetics and art education* (pp. 134–148). Urbana, IL: University of Illinois Press.

Smith, R. A. (1995). The limits and costs of integration in arts education. *Arts Education Policy Review, 96*(5), 21–25.

Smith, R. A. (2002). The new pluralism and discipline-based art education. *Arts Education Policy Review, 104*(1), 11–16.

Smith, R. A. (2004). Aesthetic education: Questions and issues. In E. W. Eisner & M. D. Day (Eds.), *Handbook of research and policy in art education* (pp. 163–86). Mahwah, NJ: Lawrence Erlbaum Associates.

Smith, R. A., & Simpson, A. (Eds.). (1991). *Aesthetics and arts education.* Urbana, IL: University of Illinois Press.

Snyder, S. (2001). Connection, correlation, and integration. *Music Educators Journal, 87*(5), 32–39, 70.

Sotiropoulou-Zormpala, M. (2012a). Reflections on aesthetic teaching: An approach to language arts in early childhood curriculum. *Art Education: The Journal of the National Art Education Association, 65*(1), 6–10.

Sotiropoulou-Zormpala, M. (2012b). Aesthetic teaching: Seeking a balance between teaching arts and teaching through the arts. *Arts Education Policy Review, 113*(4), 123–128. doi:10.1080/10632913.2012.719419

Sotiropoulou-Zormpala, M. (2016). Seeking a higher level of arts integration across the curriculum. *Arts Education Policy Review, 117*(1), 43–54. doi:10.1080/1063 2913.2014.966288

Sotiropoulou-Zormpala, M., & Mouriki-Zervou, A. (2018). Aesthetics-based arts integration in elementary education. *The International Journal of Arts Education, 13*(1), 33–44. doi:10.18848/2326-9944/CGP/v13i01/33-44.

Sotiropoulou-Zormpala, M., Trouli, K., & Linardakis, M. (2015). Arts education in Greek Universities for future pre-school and primary school teachers: Departmental programs and students' views. *Preschool and Primary Education, 3*(1), 34–52. doi:10.12681/ppej.105

Sousa, D. A., & Pilecki, T. (2013). *From stem to steam: Using brain-compatible strategies to integrate the arts.* Thousand Oaks, CA: Sage.

Spidell-Rusher, A., McGrevin, C., & Lambiotte, J. (1992). Belief systems of early childhood teachers and their principals regarding early childhood education. *Early Childhood Research Quarterly, 7*(2), 277–296.

Tafa, E. (2011). The education of preschool children and the teachers' role. In C. Chryssafidis & R. Sivropoulou (Eds.), *Principles and perspectives of preschool education* (pp. 205–232). Thessaloniki: Kiriakidis Brothers.

Tarr, P. (2001). Aesthetic codes in early childhood classrooms: What art educators can learn from Reggio Emilia. *Art Education, 54*(3), 33–39.

Tavin, K. (2005). Hauntological shifts: Fear and loathing of popular (visual) culture. *Studies in Art Education, 46*(2), 101–117.

Tavin, K., & Hausman, J. (2004). Art education and visual culture in the age of globalization. *Art Education, 57*(5), 47–53.

Tolstoy, L. (1964). What is art? In W. E. Kennick (Ed.), *Art and philosophy: Readings in aesthetics* (pp. 7–18). New York, NY: St. Martin's Press (Original work published 1897).

Upitis, R. (2011). *Arts education for the development of the whole child.* Toronto: Elementary Teachers' Federation of Ontario.

Van de Kamp, M. T., Admiraal, W., Van Drie, J., & Rijlaarsdam, G. (2015). Enhancing divergent thinking in visual arts education: Effects of explicit instruction of meta-cognition. *British Journal of Educational Psychology, 85*(1), 47–58.

Van den Akker, R., Gibbons, A., & Vermeulen, T. (Eds.). (2017). *Metamodernism: Historicity, affect and depth after postmodernism.* London: Rowman & Littlefield.

Van Leeuwen, T. (2015). Multimodality in education: Some directions and some questions. *TELOS Quarterly, 49*(3), 582–589.

Vattimo, G. (1992). *The transparent society* (D. Webb, Trans.). Cambridge, MA: Polity Press.

Vygotsky, L. S. (2004). Imagination and creativity in childhood. *Journal of Russian and East European Psychology, 42*(1), 7–97.

Walton, K. (1970). Categories of art. *The Philosophical Review, 79*, 334–367.

Webster, S., & Wolfe, M. (2013). Incorporating the aesthetic dimension into pedagogy. *Australian Journal of Teacher Education, 38*(10), 21–33. doi:10.14221/ajte.2013v38n10.2

Wellmer, A. (1984). On the dialectic of modernism and postmodernism. *Praxis International, 4*(4), 337–362.

Wenger, E. (1998). *Communities of practice: Learning, meaning, and identity.* Cambridge, MA: Harvard University Press.

White, B. (2009). *Aesthetics primer.* New York, NY: Peter Lang.

Winner, E. (2003). Beyond the evidence given: A critical commentary on Critical Links. *Arts Education Policy Review, 104*(3), 1–13.

Winner, E., & Cooper, M. (2000). Mute those claims: No evidence (yet) for a causal link between arts study and academic achievement. *The Journal of Aesthetic Education, 34*(3–4), 11–75.

Winner, E., Goldstein, T., & Vincent-Lancrin, S. (2013). *Art for art's sake? The impact of arts education.* OECD Publishing.

Wolin, R. (1984). Modernism vs. postmodernism. *Telos, 62*, 9–31.

Wright, R. (2006). Walking the walk: Review of learner-centered teaching. *Life Sciences Education, 5*(311), 311–312.

Zangwill, N. (2001). *The metaphysics of beauty.* Ithaca, NY: Cornell University Press.

Zevin, J. (2000). *Social studies for the twenty-first century: Methods and materials for teaching.* Mahwah: NJ: Lawrence Erlbaum Associates, Inc.

Ziehe, T. (2009). "Normal learning problems" in youth: In the context of underlying cultural convictions. In K. Illeris (Ed.), *Contemporary theories of learning: Learning theorists . . . in their own words* (pp. 184–199). London and New York, NY: Routledge.

Discography

Hadjidakis, M. (music), Roussos, G. (lyrics). (1970 first recording). Thalassa plateia [Wide sea]. Vinyl record: *Mythos.* Athens: Lyra.

Index

Note: Page numbers in italics indicate a figure, and page numbers in bold indicate a table on the corresponding page.